The Concept of Social Justice

The Concept of Social Justice

Edited by Christopher Wolfe

ST. AUGUSTINE'S PRESS
South Bend, Indiana

Library of Congress Control Number: 2019950732

St. Augustine's Press
www.staugustine.net

Table of Contents

Introduction
Christopher Wolfe
University of Dallas

Today we often hear the phrase "social justice," perhaps especially on college campuses. It is a welcome element of campus life in many ways, since there is a tendency for middle-class college students to become very absorbed in their own lives and not to see a larger horizon—one that calls them to service to others.

But there are also questions about the way the phrase is used. Is it desirable that "social justice" focus solely on issues such as "government programs to fight poverty," "opposing the use of military force," and "diversity" (exclusively regarding race, gender, and sexual orientation)? Government programs to fight poverty can be valuable (if they do it well); the use of military force should be avoided when possible (if there are not compelling reasons of justice to use it); and diversity can be useful (to the extent that it facilitates an appreciation of *bona fide* substantive goods). Might an exclusive or even a primary focus on such issues, however, foster a truncated view of social justice? Is it appropriate to omit or give less attention to other subjects, such as life issues (abortion and euthanasia), the sanctity of marriage, and the integrity of natural reproduction?

A broader question is the relation between general principles of social justice and specific programs to achieve those ends. For example, it is a general principle of social justice that people have access to adequate medical care, but there is a great diversity of proposals regarding the question of how to achieve this goal. Having a clear understanding of the general principles is an important first step, but without determination of concrete means there is no realization of justice in fact. Yet, are there dangers in a quick movement from general principles of "social justice" to highly controversial applications of those principles based on certain empirical judgments about which men of good will can legitimately differ—with the assumption that the latter are as authoritative elements of social justice as the former?

A deeper question about social justice might be found in the implied assumption that, for most people (those who don't directly work on issues such as poverty), "social justice" is not a significant aspect of their "ordinary" lives—their participation in the everyday world of work and business and family—but rather a matter of certain "special" acts outside the ordinary course of life (e.g., volunteer activities). That is, many people tend to compartmentalize social justice into special acts of service as opposed to integrating it into a conception of the person in his entirety and life in its entirety.

The inspiration for this book comes from the fact that current discussions of "social justice" often deal overwhelmingly with programs that aim to advance certain specific and controversial policies to deal with various social problems. In the process, important theoretical questions about social justice are not even confronted, much less resolved. For example, what does the word "social" add to "justice"? Isn't all justice "social"? What is the relation between "social justice" and more classical Aristotelian terms such as "distributive justice," "commutative justice," and "legal justice"?[1] With respect to its current usage, is the term "social justice" applicable only to special policies or programs (e.g., government or nonprofit social welfare programs)? Does it apply only to the provision of material goods and services? Does it play a role in the ordinary, everyday world of business and work?

The papers in this book aim, then, not at identifying some particular set of public policies that allegedly constitute the right content of "social justice," but at reflection on the meaning of social justice. It is not an exhortation to pursue policies that are "understood," without discussion, to be the right way to pursue social justice. It is not aimed at stimulating

---

1   This puzzle is similar to questions about what Catholics call "the social teachings" or "social doctrine" of the Church—this too is a relatively modern phrase, ordinarily used with respect to papal teachings on social and political matters since Leo XIII's *Rerum novarum*. But didn't the Church teach about social and political affairs before 1891?

activism, mobilizing people to go out and achieve social justice now. Rather, it aims at building the foundation upon which people can identify general principles of justice and make reasonable prudential judgments about how to pursue social justice. This theoretical orientation means that it is neither "right-wing" nor "left-wing."

The authors of these papers are *committed* to something like "social justice"—they don't believe that it is a spurious notion that should be rejected. They may very well disagree about exactly how to pursue social justice. But their primary concern here is to ask, simply, "what *is* social justice?"

We have to ask whether "social justice" is a new, hitherto undiscovered reality—something that fills a gap in previous philosophical and theological reflection, or at least articulates something known very imperfectly. Is it a term that is applicable to new empirical realities unknown to earlier ages (such as industrialization)? Or is it simply a new term for something already known and discussed long before the term was used—but, if so, why that new term?

The late Jean Elshtain's contribution to this volume asks whether "justice is an empty abstraction?" She notes that the thought of John Rawls has dominated recent academic thinking on justice, and that "the highly abstract and hypothetical nature of Rawls' discourse . . . tends to make the concrete steps taken to ameliorate distress and to respond to the immediate cry of justice, look rather small." But the reality is that "justice is not limited to official public policy and its outcomes, whether for good or ill. . . .Those who are called to take concrete action do not traffic in big abstractions like 'the poor' but, instead, respond to a specific set of claims in a specific set of circumstances."

She also suggests that there is a danger of overlooking a broader common commitment to social justice when we demonize those who have different ideas about the means to attain that end. "If we could debate about means rather than pitch the question as if it were a duel between the good guys and the bad, we would be more likely to come up with workable public policies that at least try to 'do no harm'," though we understand we will never achieve perfect justice.

Elshtain argues that there is no "stipulative" meaning of justice, that it is complex and varied. She is critical of "monistic" approaches that would apply one conception of justice (often state-dominated) in every part of social life and threaten legitimate American pluralism. Different political cultures should also be taken into consideration, such as the American emphasis on "the nobility and goodness of an honest day's work" that is quite different from the "state-centric" European social welfare model. Her "plea is for greater clarity and modesty, suggesting that we stand down from highly abstract discussions of social justice or 'goody-goody' evocations of social justice that are so benign as to be unbelievable and, instead, speak of how we can both do no harm and help whenever and wherever we can."

Nicholas Wolterstorff sets himself the task of exploring why "social justice" (both the term, and the thing itself) evokes so much resistance. He begins by reviewing general ideas on general justice (drawing on his *Justice: Rights and Wrongs*), and then turns to the question of what social injustice is. It is "the injustice that is wreaked on members of the community by its laws and public social practices" (or, strictly speaking, by the people responsible for them). The struggle for justice requires more than speaking out against or forestalling particular episodes of wronging—it requires speaking out against, and trying to alter or eliminate, those laws and social practices.

But, if this is what social justice is, how can anyone be opposed to it? After noting that some people are opposed to the idea of social justice because they are opposed to the idea of justice in general, Wolterstorff focuses on those who don't like the idea of social justice in particular. Some people oppose social justice because they are turned off by those whose concern for social justice is combined with a mystifying and offensive obliviousness or indifference to the injustice they are perpetrating at home—they are right to be turned off by such people, but not right to let that turn them against the idea of social justice itself. Others cannot do the social analysis that requires looking beyond particular episodes of injustice to discern regularities in these episodes and their causes—they fail to see that there can be social injustice even where intentions are good. Yet others are opposed to the idea of social justice because they think that "social justice" is a "code word for the activities of those who favor an expansive welfare state"—but "[r]ecognizing that something is a social injustice carries no implications whatsoever as to how that injustice should be remedied; in particular, it does not carry the implication that the state is the remedy of first resort."

Finally, "another source of resistance to the idea of social injustice is that such resistance is often intertwined with rejection of the charge that one is a perpetrator of social injustice," either by questioning the moral standing of the person who has issued the negative moral judgment ("who are you to say . . ."), or by insisting that the victims' plight is their own fault or that nothing can be done about it. "Acknowledging that one is complicit in social injustice requires that one commit oneself to desist from the practice or reform it, if either of those is possible; and often that's more than a person can bring himself to do. . . . The reason social justice movements are almost always conflictual is that those who benefit from the status quo find the price of change too high."

The late Michael Novak first surveys common (especially academic) understandings of social justice: e.g., distribution, equality, and (defective understandings of) the common good. He also describes the way in which the term has been used simply as shorthand for the Progressive agenda, or compassion. All of these meanings, he argues, are either very inadequate understandings or widely misunderstood. In examining earlier usage of the term, especially by Leo XIII, he emphasizes that social justice cannot be identified with "equality." Rather, social justice emerged as a response to the need for a new virtue in modern economic circumstances, a virtue related to the capacity to work together, to cooperate in the activity of associations.

John Finnis begins by looking at the term "social justice" as first used in documents of the Catholic magisterium by Pius XI (*Quadragesimo anno*), contrasting it with its use by John Stuart Mill. He asks why Pius XI felt the need to go beyond the typical Aristotelean-Thomistic division of justice into "distributive" and "commutative."

Finnis traces the emergence of modern "social justice" to a misstatement of St. Thomas' conception of justice by one of his great commentators, Cajetan. Thomas, following Aristotle, distinguishes between general (or legal) justice, and two particular forms of justice, commutative and distributive. Cajetan describes three kinds of particular justice: legal (dealing with the relation of the parts to the whole), commutative (dealing with the relation of the parts to each other), and distributive (dealing with the relation of the whole to the parts).

As an Italian scholar (Giorgio del Vecchio) noted in 1946, it was the eclipse of Aquinas' category or conception of legal—that is, general—justice, and its replacement (under the same name) with a much thinner category and conception focused on the citizen's duty as subject, that stimulated nineteenth-century thinkers, and in due course Pius XI and his advisers, to fill the gap with the new term. "Social justice is thus, like Aquinas' legal justice, a responsibility in the first instance of law and government, bearing on private property and transactions, and directed towards securing the common good of the political community." This conception of social justice, oriented toward a common good that considers worth and need, as well as equality, is "far distant from the loose modern idea of social justice as something that can be read off from the depiction or structure of a state of affairs, so that the sheer fact of wide disparities of (say) wealth or educational attainment can be declared to be in itself contrary to social justice."

Joseph Koterski, S.J., argues that documents such as *Caritas in veritate* (Benedict XVI's third encyclical) and the International Theological Commission's "In Search of a Universal Ethic: A New Look at the Natural Law" not only re-affirm the importance of social justice within the corpus of Catholic social teaching, but also insist on the need to correct an unfortunate tendency. That tendency is the isolation within separate "silos"—rather than a unified integration—of the three substantive areas of Catholic social doctrine: the economic, the political, and the cultural (including marriage, family, and society). This silo approach may have been inadvertently encouraged by the tendency of magisterial documents to focus on one particular area of concern, and especially by the confinement of some social encyclicals to economic questions.

Fr. Koterski emphasizes that the documents on the Church's social teaching (especially the social encyclicals) have to be read in the context of their historical unfolding. A sensitive understanding of that evolution will observe the fundamental continuity of the teaching, while also recognizing ways in which later documents serve as correctives to certain aspects of earlier ones.

A detailed analysis of Benedict's encyclical and the ITC document on natural law leads to three conclusions: 1) the duties of social justice flow from a proper understanding of the common good (as opposed to, say, philosophical egalitarianism); 2) social justice concerns are an important part of the state's administration of justice, being rooted in the common good, including especially the traditional teaching on the "universal destination" of the goods of the earth; and 3) the distinction between obligations of social justice and social charity emphasized by Benedict is rooted in the classical Augustinian understanding of "the two cities."

Robert G. Kennedy's chapter considers "the foundations of the Church's teaching on the good society, how an evolving notion of social justice has moved beyond those foundations, and how a renewed appreciation of the importance of charity can restore practical integrity to the Church's teaching." He distinguishes three stages of Catholic social justice. First, Leo XIII confronted the question of "how to reconceive modern society, in the light of the Gospel, as an organic unity in the face of so many dislocations caused by political, economic and intellectual revolutions" and his encyclicals "constituted not so much an alternative to Liberalism and Socialism as a deeper, more comprehensive and more realistic conception of a good society that continues to serve as a foundation for the Church's social doctrine."

Second, however, many Catholic thinkers subsequently embraced key Liberal or Socialist premises, working hard to reconcile these premises with Leo's teaching and gradually shaping a theory of social justice that moved the Catholic social tradition in a new direction. Departing from Leo's realism, they adopted the view that "social structures could, and must be, engineered and that the dominant goal of action in society was the establishment of a right ordering of these structures, which ordering would constitute a sort of abstract justice." A particularly important figure in the U.S. was Msgr. John A. Ryan, who created a blend of Catholic social doctrine and Progressivism, with more expansive views about the role government could play.

Third, building on the work of Ryan and others, a new stage—the Modern Catholic Vision of social justice—emerged and has been dominant since the 1960s. This view has an expanded notion of public goods, and its objective is "the re-ordering of society so that a set of new structures (laws, regulations, policies and practices) is put in place that will ensure a desirable distribution of public goods." On this view, the role of charity is limited, being "a motivation for Christians to pursue the larger work of social justice or . . . a local act of immediate relief, with the larger work of addressing the causes of distress left to the pursuit of social justice." Kennedy argues that Benedict XVI's *Caritas in veritate* aims to recover a larger and more central role for charity in Catholic social teaching.

Brian Benestad examines how the United States Conference of Catholic Bishops (USCCB) has chosen to make its contribution to the political community, and offers some reflections on their mode of engagement in the light of Catholic social doctrine. He notes Benedict XVI's characterization of the Church's role: it is "simply to help purify reason and to contribute, here and now, to the acknowledgment and attainment of what is just." As part of that work of purifying reason "the Church forms the conscience of people, builds their character, and motivates them to act justly." The Church thus *indirectly* contributes to the achievement of justice—especially by the action of the laity in temporal affairs, but without the Church becoming engaged in partisan matters on which the faithful can legitimately differ.

Benestad notes, however, that since the 1960s the USCCB has continually taken a wide range of partisan stands. He argues that the reasons proffered for acting this way are not convincing, and that, in fact, they do great harm, by confusing the laity on the distinction between authoritative and non-authoritative teaching. This is by no means "a call for the Church to withdraw from the public arena," but rather to have "an even deeper impact on American culture and public policy, but to do so as Church."

He buttresses his analysis with a careful reading of two "Faithful Citizenship" documents of the USCCB. The 2003 "Faithful Citizenship" relied heavily on the "consistent life ethic" promoted by Cardinal Joseph Bernardin and provided inadequate guidance to the faithful because it failed to make distinctions between moral evils of greatly different magnitude. The later document—"Forming Consciences for Faithful Citizenship" (2007)—still continued to include many non-authoritative episcopal statements on partisan policies, but it (together with "Catholics in Political Life" [2004]) made significant improvements over the earlier one, especially by emphasizing the difference between political matters that implicate intrinsically evil acts and those that do not.

What are some of the lessons of this book? The essays in this book suggest at least the following:

1) the term "social justice" so often invoked today is often vague and imprecise—the resources that can give it more precision are available, though unfortunately not widely known;

2) the misuse of social justice is no excuse for rejecting the concept entirely—there is a core notion of social justice that is an essential component of the common good;

3) the identification of "social justice" with a particular political program (most commonly, of the Left) is unjustifiable—at its best, social justice lays down essential general principles that need to guide concrete efforts to pursue the common good, but that also leave considerable leeway for differences among people of good will;

4) the "openness" of social justice to different modes of achieving the common good—the acknowledgment of a legitimate pluralism of views about the specific content of social justice—is not a valid excuse for ignoring the important demands it makes upon us, failing (by omission) to give it the importance it merits;

5) the tendency to identify social justice overwhelmingly with government programs (discounting, for example, the resources of civil society) is mistaken—though it is also true that a *prima facie* hostility to government programs would be mistaken;

6) anyone committed to social justice should not focus merely on political and economic structures, but should see the formation of moral character and consciences as central to the struggle for social justice;

7) it is seriously misleading to identify social justice simply with economic issues, failing to see the deep interconnections between economic and other political and cultural issues, including especially family and life issues;

8) justice and charity should never be seen as opposed or alternative ways to approach social problems, but rather as deeply intertwined and interdependent perspectives.

Most of the essays in this book were delivered as papers at an American Public Philosophy Institute conference held at Marquette University in the fall of 2010, which was made possible by a generous grant from the Earhart Foundation, whose support is gratefully acknowledged.

Chapter One

Is Social Justice an Empty Abstraction?

Jean Bethke Elshtain

University of Chicago and Georgetown University

"Social justice" has become a mantra, an abstraction, even a litmus test separating the good guys from the bad. One hears the term "social justice" from pulpit and podium, in article and argument, in policy and propaganda. So much so that its meaning—whatever that may be or may have been—is an out-of-focus picture, blurry; there's no "there" there, so to speak.

A backdrop to this confusion is the influence of the late John Rawls on discussions of justice. The Rawlsian imperative has dominated legal and academic discussion of "justice" for decades. Perhaps it is time to move on. Given the highly abstract and hypothetical nature of Rawls' discourse, it tends to make the concrete steps taken to ameliorate distress and to respond to the immediate cry of justice look rather small.

How do we account for the fact that, on the ground, social justice is often enjoined but rarely joined, as in: "What do you mean, exactly, concretely? What can we really do? What can I do?" Within the Rawlsian framework, the hopes and demands are couched at such a removed level that it is difficult to determine where individual moral agency enters. There is also the suggestion, one that should surely be problematic for Christians, that if one subsumes *caritas* into public policy, the requirements of neighbor-love will be satisfied.

Perhaps a brief story will help to illustrate these concerns. About a year after the catastrophe of Hurricane Katrina, I participated in a meeting in the Netherlands that brought together thinkers from Europe, the United States, and beyond. After the panel in which I had participated, and in light of where the discussion had gone in general, a distinguished scholar and academic stated quite confidently that the reason that Katrina was such a horror was the fact that it displayed a "failure of solidarity" in the United States. Had I had the opportunity to respond, I would have argued, to the contrary, that Katrina was a brilliant example of solidarity in action.

Here's why my view and his are so radically different. My interlocutor saw as legitimate in a crisis only public policy, only government action— witnessing the inefficiency and the confusion among local, state, and federal authorities made it difficult to sort out where aid would go and how it would get there, given the fact that the local authorities in New Orleans governed, if that is a legitimate word to use, a city that is known for its corruption. So you not only saw public authority breaking down, but you saw authority participating in the chaos.

What this distinguished scholar missed—and what did not get the lion's share of media attention because the media was out to demonize the Bush Administration, as the media narrative seems to require its villains—was the extraordinary outpouring from civil society. And the heart of American civil society is our churches. In Nashville, Tennessee, I traveled to a drop-off point with a load of canned goods, blankets and bedding, and clothing to deliver, only to discover that they were so overwhelmed with donations they could not accept any more. They had received word from New Orleans that they couldn't get all the contributions distributed rapidly enough.

Through its churches, Nashvillians sponsored displaced families, taking them into their homes; schools opened themselves to displaced students and stretched their already thin resources to provide supplies and after-school tutoring; doctors and dentists offered *gratis* care. The list goes on and on. This is civil society in action. But so many are so wedded to a state-centric social welfare model, it appears to count for nothing or for very little indeed. If the state isn't taking care of things from the top down, it isn't being done.

How does that fit into my concern about "empty abstraction"? I hope you can see the fit: within a grand theory of what social justice is or requires, the Katrina situation looks like a total fiasco. But if one looks at social justice as a concrete matter of both preventing harm and helping whenever you can—St. Augustine's two rough and ready rules for the moral life—you get a different picture. Whatever the breakdowns of official governmental authority on whatever level, human beings responded to the cry for justice, to the needy, the displaced, the hungry.

Surely this is justice in action. Justice is not limited to official public policy and its outcomes, whether for good or ill.

Those who are called to take concrete action do not traffic in big abstractions like "the poor" but, instead, respond to a specific set of claims in a specific set of circumstances. To the extent that "the poor" get affixed to "social justice" as the overwhelming occasion for a focus on such justice, one is in danger of reifying the category, making it a permanent feature of discourse, put in there repeatedly and, eventually, formulaically.

But "the poor" in a given circumstance could well be a solidly middle-class family driven from their home by natural disaster. In Katrina, when we look at the hard data, we find that there was no lopsided figure of deaths by race—only a small percentage of difference between white and black deaths—but one got the distinct impression that this was not the case, that a particular group had been uniquely singled out somehow in this disaster. I suspect that by placing people in a category prior to anything having happened, we simply assume that our expectations are fulfilled.

This invites not only reification but sentimentality about the poor, as if they might be repositories of virtue or understanding unavailable to others. Human nature being what it is, this cannot be the case, of course. No one is exempt from folly, avarice, and all the rest. And if poverty has the effects on people it is alleged to have, many among the poor will likely not be awfully pleasant people—they will be limited in their horizons, perhaps grasping in their behavior, perhaps manipulative in using their status to tap liberal guilt in their favor. If poverty is as bad as we say it is, and it has the debilitating effects we claim, this is likely to be the case.

There is some truth to the Nietzschean notion that a dynamic may come into play in which one group requires another group to be unfortunate and weak in order that they remain the beneficiaries of our concern and our largesse. It follows that one perpetuates the situation rather than working to remedy it, for it gives one an identity and purpose: it does that for both sides, actually.

Those who take concrete action in times of distress are more likely to want to stop the harm, first, and then to help as best they can in order that those now harmed will not be harmed in the future—they will not be part of that permanent category, "the poor."

I won't get into all of the many problems with determining who constitutes the poor. Social scientists have been parsing this for decades. What I am trying to do is to break through the crust of "social justice" in order to probe more forthrightly into what exactly we are talking about and what exactly we are called upon to do. It is far, far easier to sit on the sidelines advocating an abstract vision of social justice than to roll up one's sleeves and put oneself on the line concretely for another human being.

Our churches present an interesting picture, then, do they not, being the mainstay of American civil society and inspiring people to concrete action and, at the same time, issuing statements by denominations, offering words from the pulpit, prayers and injunctions, that repeat the abstract mantra of "social justice."

To restate: What do we mean? Do we mean access to public goods? Do we mean equal opportunity? Do we mean massive redistribution with the state growing ever more powerful and dictating to civil society? Do we mean leveling, so that any marks of distinction are to be rejected and enjoined? Do we mean narrowing the gap between the well-to-do and others or eliminating it entirely?

A distinguished philosopher said to me, many years ago now, that neither I nor any other human being would want to live in a world of absolute justice. It would be a cruel, unforgiving world. What prompted his comment was my heated defense of "social justice" in that mantra-type way. I didn't really understand the message at first but, later, I caught a glimpse of the meaning. If justice is meted out, where lies mercy? Where is forgiveness? Are we all to get our desserts? But who deserves what and why? Do I harm my own family in order to "do" for others? If I put my family first, am I guilty of ignoring the cries of justice?

I suspect the philosopher had in mind the tendency of "justice" to be cast in such a way that it lies on one side of a divide and injustice on the other, and this comes to measure political purity. The side of injustice is represented as so malign, so beyond the pale, that it is portrayed as the side that actually takes pleasure in harming others, that revels in maldistribution and the like.

If, however, we were more modest, understanding what Reinhold Niebuhr taught some years ago now—namely, that we can agree on a basic good, that we all want justice, but this implies no agreement whatsoever on means—we will be less ready to cast some into the outer darkness, politically speaking. When one moves from the shared "good" to how to achieve it, one gets less and less concurrence.

A strong liberal may insist that the only way to get justice is to impose a draconian taxation system to denude the well-to-do and redistribute their wealth to the poor (although we'll have to disguise that we're doing this, most likely). A strong conservative may say that the only way to get more justice is to let the market work, because then more jobs are created and more people flourish (and we'll disguise the fact that those who fall by the wayside may be there through no fault of their own—they may have tried and failed—and do we care for them not at all?). Clearly, each approach carries with it unattractive unintended consequences. The point for now is that to call one side "pro" or "anti" justice would be unfair; or to call one group more "Christian" then the other is to perpetuate an injustice.

If we could debate about means rather than pitch the question as if it were a duel between the good guys and the bad, we would be more likely to come up with workable public policies that at least try to "do no harm," knowing that we will never—it is just not in the scheme of things—arrive at a moment of perfect justice, whatever one's criterion for justice may be.

This states the heart of what I wanted to say, my basic plaint. But let's probe just a bit further. Let's begin with justice itself. Despite attempts by political thinkers, both historically and currently, justice has no stipulative meaning. If you look at the history of political thought, it is a complex and varied story. Justice is understood as giving people their due. Or it is defined as equality, with equality itself construed as a kind of leveling. Or justice is reserved to the level of civic status: we are all equal as citizens and there is no presumption of equality in any other sphere—there human freedom works things out one way or another. Justice is also deployed as a weapon used by the weak against the strong—a way to beat up those who do well and drag them into mediocrity. Or justice is basic fairness—procedural fairness: we have a set of shared rules, we live by them, and the outcome is justice, whatever it is.

For Christians in particular, Jesus of Nazareth left behind no comprehensive "theory of justice." He did leave behind parables and commands to his followers: that they would feed the hungry and provide shelter for the homeless, that they would walk the extra mile for the poor and distressed. But we know that real economies do not work like God's economy of plenty (not scarcity), that is, the world beautifully limned by Jesus' feeding of the five thousand: the fish and loaves increased with distribution.

There is something beautiful and peaceful in this vision. One should hold it dear. But it is not a prescription for public policy. It can be seen, reasonably I believe, as a warning against approaching the world at every turn through a strong presupposition of "scarcity"—there isn't enough, so I'll get mine before someone else does. Primarily the Scripture calls upon us to undertake the requirement of *caritas*. And Scripture lifts up "Lazarus, who was poor," for our consideration. God loves and cherishes him; he, too, is marked by the *imago dei*. Lazarus is not someone one would likely invite into one's home. But Christians are enjoined not to leave others behind and outside the circle of concern.

Now take this teaching into the public square where one finds competing understandings of justice. You learn that justice is an essentially contested concept, one of those concepts that helps to constitute political and social life and contestation about that life, as people essentially disagree about what justice is and what justice requires. There is no knock-down argument to settle the case.

Any attempt to solve the problem of justice formulaically, borrowing from micro- or macroeconomics, ignores political realities and the myriad ways that people respond to the cries for justice in their own communities and around the world. Only what is accomplished on the level of the state apparently counts. And yet we are taught to be wary—or we should be— of an excess of concentration of power on the top. Where does this leave us?

Some would say that only a thoroughgoing overhaul culminating in secure state domination can do the job. There are those who have gone so far as to insist that this vision of justice penetrate into the interstices of the home, of marriage and the family, as homemakers receive checks directly from their husbands' employers or from the state, not for work they have done for the employers, but for work they have done at home. The mind boggles at such unmanageable and ill-conceived prospects. Beyond that, such proposals freeze women into domestic roles—or would have. It seemed odd for prospects of this sort to be advanced by feminists, both liberal and Marxist, given that they also routinely condemned the state as an instrument exclusively designed to promote "patriarchy."

But there is a very different response, one that is more humble and that remains appropriately wary of concentrating too much power on the top. It is a stance that looks more like Michael Walzer's "Spheres of Justice" than John Rawls' "Theory of Justice." Those familiar with the works of each will recall that Walzer argued, *contra* Rawls, that there was no overarching meta-theory of justice to be had; that justice functioned differently in different spheres of life (if, indeed, the word played a key role at all); that there was no one-size-fits-all, in other words. It followed that we should take some care and should refrain from what I will call a "monist approach"—the monistic demand that justice, stipulatively defined, must pertain to each and every level of society and in the same way.

Further, advancing such a notion of justice would constitute a major assault on American pluralism, on the idea of plural possibilities and institutions. We would not permit institutions to organize themselves according to their own lights and rules (within the bounds of minimal decency, of course). In the name of justice and equality, the state would feel obliged to intrude to force the Orthodox Church to make women priests or Catholic hospitals to perform abortions. Does justice demand this sort of assault against persons of conscience who are following the truth of their faith as they understand it?

If the "truth of one's faith" demanded a community that enslaved a particular group, of course, there would be an overriding imperative to intervene as basic civic rights would be violated in an egregious way. But, surely, one of the glories of the American republic has been its ability to sustain and to contain pluralities. We might wind up with a more just society on some abstract standard of measurement if we adopted the monist approach, but it would be a radically impoverished society as monism swamped difference, undermined plural possibilities.

Finally, let's say something about particular political cultures, another factor often lost in evocations of social justice. I recall well the comments of a distinguished academic working in the United States, who was wedded to the state-centric European social welfare model, the very system that is now collapsing in Europe. I suggested to him that you could not push that kind of system in the United States, that we had a quite different political culture, one far more wary of the state and far more wedded to the nobility and goodness of an honest day's work. So many fled to our shores seeking work—wanting justice, fairness, in remuneration for that work. You could not convince the majority of Americans that some cradle-to-grave welfare system is the way to go because they believe a glory of our system is its meritocratic dimension: if you are capable and work hard, you can get ahead, you can leave a better world to your children. It is unsurprising, then, that so many Americans on welfare report feeling badly about such dependence on the dole—they want to work, they want the dignity of labor.

Surely we don't want a system in which the cry of neighbor-love is responded to automatically, as it were, with some public policy or another. We know that, no matter how many agencies you set up, how many laws you pass, and all the rest, things will go astray; that the unintended consequences of social change are sometimes so great they swamp the change itself; that the cry of the neighbor should not be settled with a vote but with a hand out and a hand up.

In conclusion, my plea is for greater clarity and modesty, suggesting that we stand down from highly abstract discussions of social justice or "goody-goody" evocations of social justice that are so benign as to be unbelievable and, instead, speak of how we can both do no harm and help whenever and wherever we can.

Chapter Two
All Justice Is Social—
But Not All Justice Is Social Justice

Nicholas Wolterstorff

Yale University

Institute of Advanced Studies in Culture,

University of Virginia

The term "social justice" is the site of controversy. For some people it expresses their mission in life. For others it evokes images of busybody do-goodism and intrusive government. I want to explore why the term evokes resistance—and not only why the term does, but why the thing itself does, namely, social justice. But before we can do that, we'll have to identify the sort of justice that social justice is. And in order to do that, I will to have to explain what I take justice as such to be. My explanation of the nature of justice will be a brief exposition of the way of thinking about justice that I develop at length in my book, *Justice: Rights and Wrongs*.[1]

I

A well-known formula for justice handed down to us from antiquity comes from the ancient Roman jurist Ulpian: justice is rendering to each his or her *ius*—that is, his or her right, his or her due. Ulpian's formula is a definition of the virtue of justice. Justice itself is present in society insofar as each person is rendered what he or she has a right to.

---

1   Princeton: Princeton University Press, 2008.

Notice that Ulpian is tacitly distinguishing between having or possessing a right, and being rendered that right—or as I will sometimes say, *enjoying* that right. Not being rendered one's right does not mean that one does not possess that right. It means that one is not enjoying a right that one possesses, that one is being deprived of it, not being rendered it. If one has or possesses a certain right, then one may either be rendered that right or deprived of it. In the former case, one enjoys that to which one has a right; in the latter case, one is wronged. Being wronged is the dark side of having a right, just as guilt is the dark side of obligation. The person who does not enjoy her right is wronged, the person who does not do what she ought to do is guilty.

To have or possess a right is not to stand in the relation of possession to some metaphysically mysterious entity called "a right." Having a right consists of having a right *to* something; it makes no sense to say that one has a certain right but that there is nothing to which one has that right. To have or possess a right is to stand to something which is not a right in the relation of *having a right to* it. The whole term, "having a right to," expresses the relation. The indefinite article "a" does no work; one might as well say, "having right to."

The relation is, of course, a normative relation. To stand to something in the relation of *having (a) right to* it is to stand to it in the relation of *having legitimate claim to* it. Or to express the idea in yet a third way, it is to stand to it in the relation of its *being due* one. Let's first consider the sort of thing to which one can stand in this relationship, and then consider the nature of the relation itself.

That to which one can stand in the relation of having (a) right to it is, in the first place, some state or event in one's life that is or would be a good in one's life, a life-good.[2] Admittedly it's not always evident from how we

---

2 This statement requires a qualification that, on this occasion, I will not insert into the text. There are certain ways of depriving me of life such that I have the right against my fellow human beings to the good of their not depriving me of life in those ways. (This may be a *prima facie* right, not an *ultima facie* right; and it may be a right that one can forfeit.) So consider the good to which I have that right, the good of their not depriving me of life in those ways. This is obviously a good that *pertains to* my life; but it is not, strictly speaking, a good *in* my life. That is to say, it is not a state or event *in* my life that contributes positively to its estimability. It was a question put to me by Chris Eberle that led me to see the need for this qualification.

speak about rights that this is true. We speak, for example, of having a right to a seat on the plane; and a seat on a plane is not a state or event in one's life. But if we look beneath the words to the structure of the situation, we'll see that what I said is true. What we refer to as a right to a seat on the plane is more fully described as a right to *take* a seat on the plane. And taking a seat on the plane is an event in one's life; more specifically, it's an event that is or would be a good in one's life. Of course, enjoying one's right to take a seat on the plane might have disastrous consequences; the plane might crash. In that case, the whole package, taking a seat on the plane and the plane's crashing, is a bad thing in one's life; but that doesn't make the thing itself to which one had a right, namely, taking a seat on the plane, a bad thing.

And now for an important step in the argument: those life-goods to which one has a right are always ways of being treated that are or would be a good in one's life. That to which one has a right is always to the good of being treated a certain way. Normally it's to the good of being treated a certain way by others; in the limiting case, it's to the good of being treated a certain way by oneself. It will simplify our discussion if we set that limiting case off to the side and say that that to which one has a right is always some good of being treated a certain way by others.[3]

Here, too, it's not always evident from our way of speaking about rights that this is true. I have a right to walk on the Charlottesville Mall. But my walking on the Charlottesville Mall is not something others do to me; it's something I do. If we look beneath the words to the structure of the situation, however, we will see that my right to walk on the Charlottesville Mall is my right *to be free* to walk on the Mall without hindrance.[4] And

---

3 Third-party rights constitute an exception to this principle: I may have a right against you to your treating Mary a certain way rather than to your treating me a certain way. This would be the case if you promised me that you would extend some benefit to Mary. Continually taking account of this sort of exception in the text would unnecessarily complicate the discussion.

4 The distinction between claim-rights and permission-rights is indispensable here; our topic throughout is claim-rights. My claim-right to walk on the Charlottesville Mall is my right to be free to walk on the Mall without hindrance. My permission-right to walk on the Mall consists of its being permissible for me to walk on the Mall. Whereas a claim-right is a right *to be treated* a certain way, a permission-right is a right *to do* something.

being free to walk on the Mall without hindrance is a way of being treated by others. So too, though taking a seat on the plane is something one does, not a way of being treated by others, if we look more closely we see that the right in question is the right *to be allowed* to take a seat on the plane; and that is a way of being treated by others.

Earlier I said that rights are normative relationships. What we can now add is that rights are normative *social* relationships; that to which one has a right is always to the good of being treated a certain way by one's fellows. It takes at least two to have a right—with the exception of those cases in which one has a right to being treated a certain way by oneself.

If Ulpian was right—and I think he was—that justice consists of enjoying that to which one has (a) right, then what can now be said is that justice is present in society insofar as the members of society stand to each other in the normative social relationship of being treated as they have a right to be treated.

We now face what I regard as the most challenging point for anyone trying to construct a theory of justice, namely, explaining the nature of the relation of *having a right to*. Though that to which one has a right is always a way of being treated by others that is or would be a good in one's life, the converse is not the case: there are many ways of being treated by others that would be a good in one's life but to which one does not have a right. I think it would be a great good in my life were I to be given a Rembrandt painting to hang on my living room wall, along with a security force to stand guard. But I don't have a right to that life-good; my not enjoying that good does not imply that I am wronged. So what accounts for the fact that, of those ways of being treated by others that would be a good in one's life, one has a right to some and not to others?

Obviously some of our rights are bestowed on us by legislation or social practice, or generated in us by some such speech act as promising. I have a right to receive a monthly Social Security check from the U.S. government on account of the Social Security legislation passed in the 1930s—plus the fact that I possess the qualifications specified in the legislation. But not all my rights are like that. Some are *natural* rights. Wholly apart from legislation, social practices, and speech acts, I have a right to not being murdered, to not being tortured for the pleasure of the torturer, to not being insulted or demeaned. So what accounts for the fact that, of those ways of being treated by others that would be a good in one's life, one has a *natural* right to some of those ways of being treated while, to others, one either has no right or only a socially bestowed or generated right?

The view on this point that is presently dominant in the literature is that natural rights are all either specifications of, or conditions for the enjoyment of, our fundamental natural right to autonomy—that is, our fundamental natural right to form for ourselves a plan of life and to enact that plan, revising it along the way as seems appropriate.

Popular though this theory is, I think it has to be rejected. One problem confronting the theory is explaining what that purported right to autonomy comes to. Clearly nobody has the right to do whatever he or she sees fit to do; so what then is that purported natural right from which every other natural right is thought to follow either as a specification of the right or as a condition for enjoying it? I judge that no autonomy theorist has succeeded in answering that question.

But we don't have to get into the interminable discussions surrounding the nature of autonomy to see that the theory won't do. Everybody reading this essay will agree that to torture imprisoned criminals as a way of punishing them is to wrong them; they have a right not to be punished by torture. To employ torture as a means of punishment is to treat them unjustly. But what makes it wrong is not that their autonomy is thereby impaired. Their autonomy is already impaired; they are locked up. What's wrong about torturing them, I would say, is that their dignity as human beings is violated. And in general, it's my view that natural rights are grounded in worth, in dignity. I have a right to the life-good of being treated a certain way by others just in case, were I not treated that way, I would be treated with under-respect for my worth, my dignity.

Rights, so understood, represent an interweaving of life-goods, on the one hand, and of the worth or dignity of the human beings whose life-goods those are, on the other hand. Any ethical theory that works only with life-goods, and not also with the worth or dignity of human beings, is incapable of giving an account of natural rights. Modern utilitarianism is one such theory; eudaimonism, currently enjoying a renaissance, is another. One does not get rights by piling up life-goods. The fact that having a Rembrandt painting hanging on my living room wall would be an enormous good in my life and in the lives of others does not bring it about that I have a right to that good.

One last point must be made here, namely, that rights have peremptory or trumping force. Let me develop the point in a slightly roundabout way that will prove useful later in our discussion.

Kant introduced the concept of an imperfect duty: a duty that one has is an imperfect duty just in case it is a duty to treat someone or other in such-and-such a way but there is no person such that it is one's duty to treat *that* person in that way. An example would be my duty when walking in Manhattan to be charitable to beggars on the street. It's my duty to extend charity to some beggar or other; but there is no beggar such that it is my duty to extend charity to him.[5]

Now let's introduce, as the mirror image of this concept of an imperfect duty, the concept of an imperfect right. A right that one has is imperfect just in case it is the right to be treated a certain way by someone or other but there is no one such that one has the right against *that* person to his treating one in that way. A beggar in Manhattan has the right to receive charity from one or another of the well-to-do people on the street; but there is no one such that it is against *that* person that he has the right.[6]

Let us now set imperfect duties and imperfect rights off to the side for the time being. We can then formulate the following *Principle of Correlatives* for the relation between perfect duties and perfect rights:

> A person A has an *ultima facie* right against a person B to B's treating him in such-and-such a way if and only if B has an *ultima facie* duty toward A to treat him in that way.

Hassan has an *ultima facie* right against Randall to Randall's not torturing him if and only if Randall has an *ultima facie* duty toward Hassan to refrain from torturing him.

---

5   A duty can also be imperfect in that one has a duty to treat a particular person in some way or other within a certain range, but not a duty to treat him in any particular way within that range. For example, I may have a duty to alleviate a particular person's poverty in some way or other, without having the duty to do so in any particular way.

6   A right can also be imperfect in that one has a right against a particular person that he treat one in some way or other within a certain range—to alleviate one's poverty in some way or other, for example—but not a right to his treating one in any particular way within that range.

Now suppose I have an *ultima facie* duty toward you to refrain from torturing you and that you have an *ultima facie* right against me to my not torturing you. But suppose I can bring about a large number of goods in the lives of people by torturing you. What should I do, all things considered?

I should refrain from torturing you. It's not always the case that something I should do is something I am obligated to do; it may be that I should apply for a certain job even though I'm not obligated to apply. But if, all things considered, I ought to perform a certain action, then I should perform it, period. It makes no sense to say that I ought to do it but that it's not something I should do. Obligation trumps. And if obligation trumps, then rights trump—by virtue of the principle of correlatives. If Hassan has an *ultima facie* right to Randall's not torturing him, then not torturing him is what Randall should do—no matter how many goods Randall might bring about by torturing Hassan.

II

That completes the presentation of my way of thinking about justice and rights. It's time to turn our attention to social justice.

What is social justice? As we go about trying to discover the answer to this question, let's keep in mind that we are dealing here with only a part of justice. It's an extremely important part, but it's not the whole.

The Old Testament prophets were the first great spokesmen for social justice in what has come to be the Western tradition. Taking a look at the structure of what they said will prove to be a good way of getting hold of the idea. Here, from Isaiah, is a typical passage:

> Woe to those who decree iniquitous decrees,
> and the writers who keep writing oppression,
> to turn aside the needy from justice
> and to rob the poor of my people of their right,
> that widows may be their spoil,
> and that they may make the fatherless their prey!
> What will you do on the day of punishment,
> in the storm which will come from afar?

To whom will you turn for help,
and where will you leave your wealth? (Isa. 10:1–3)

Biting words. Even more biting are the following words, also from Isaiah:

The Lord said:
Because the daughters of Zion are haughty
 and walk with outstretched necks,
 glancing wantonly with their eyes,
mincing along as they go,
 tinkling with their feet;
the Lord will smite with a scab
 the heads of the daughters of Zion,
 and the Lord will lay bare their secret parts.

In that day the Lord will take away the finery of the anklets, the headbands, and the crescents; the pendants, the bracelets, and the scarves; the head-dresses, the armlets, the sashes, the perfume boxes, and the amulets; the signet rings and nose rings; the festal robes, the mantles, the cloaks, and the handbags; the garments of gauze, the linen garments, the turbans, and the veils.

Instead of perfume there will be rottenness;
 and instead of a girdle, a rope;
and instead of well-set hair, baldness,
 and instead of a rich robe, a girding of sackcloth;
 instead of beauty, shame.
Your men shall fall by the sword
 and your mighty men in battle. (Isa. 3:16–25)

Notice, first, that Isaiah does not mention any particular episodes of injustice or any particular wrongdoers. He and the other prophets were not hesitant to point the finger when the occasion arose; recall the prophet Nathan confronting King David for his affair with Bathsheba with the accusing words, "You are the man." The target of Isaiah's attack in these passages is not specific episodes of injustice and specific wrongdoers; his target is laws and public social practices whose effect is to turn aside widows, orphans, and the poor from justice and to rob them of their right.

I suggest that we are touching here on the central feature of that special form of injustice which is social injustice. Social injustice is the injustice that is wreaked on members of the community by its laws and public social practices. Of course, strictly speaking it is not the laws that wreak the injustice but those who pass and enforce the laws, and strictly speaking it is not the practices that wreak the injustice but those who engage in the practices.

To recognize social injustice one must be able to look beyond particular episodes of injustice, and beyond particular wrongdoers and victims, to recognize a certain pattern in a number of episodes. That done, one must then be able to look behind those patterns to discern what accounts for them, namely, certain laws and public social practices. This latter ability, the ability to discern the cause of the pattern of injustice, requires the ability to engage in a certain kind of abstraction. To determine whether someone is a participant in a public social practice that wreaks injustice one must be able to abstract from his intentions. A person may wrong someone without intending to do so. We'll be coming back to this point later.

Some people find it difficult, both in their own case and in the case of others, to perform the sort of abstraction required for recognizing social injustice. This is not how they normally think. Others find it not so much difficult to think this way as offensive to be told that they and their friends are perpetrating injustice. They are good people with the best of intentions. "If the prophet Isaiah thinks that Asher and Benjamin did something wrong to someone, then he should have the courage to name them and point his finger at them. He should not use a wide brush that tars good people along with bad."

Given the understanding of social *in*-justice that I have just now spelled out, it's tempting to say that social justice is present in a society when there is no social *in*-justice in that society, that is, when no one is being treated unjustly by the laws and public social practices. But that's not how the term "social justice" is ordinarily used. It is ordinarily used to refer to the actions of speaking up in opposition to social injustice and struggling to undo it. Social justice organizations are organizations that oppose social injustice.

So that's how I will use the term.[7] When it's the laws and public social practices of society that lead to members of the community being robbed of their rights, the struggle for justice requires more than speaking out against particular episodes of wronging and more than trying to forestall such episodes. It requires speaking out against, and trying to alter or eliminate, those laws and social practices. And that is social justice.

In focusing the fire of his critique on iniquitous laws and public social practices, the prophet assumes that things can be different. The extant laws and practices are not laws of nature ordained by God; neither do they express the ineluctable laws of the marketplace or the unalterable preconditions of social order. The prophets do not think of the widows, the orphans, and the impoverished as social unfortunates about whom there is nothing to be done; they think of them as the victims of laws and practices that can be changed. It is sometimes said that not until the early modern period did people in general believe that social structures and practices are human constructs that can be changed. It seems to me unmistakable that the Hebrew prophets already believed that.

Not only does the prophetic critique of social injustice assume that the laws and public social practices of society *can* be changed; it assumes they *ought to* be changed. The prophetic critique assumes that there is a moral standard outside these laws and practices by which they are to be judged, and it declares that they fail to meet that standard. The laws and practices are not a standard unto themselves. The fact that this is how we do things in our society does not make those things just. Justice transcends our laws and practices. The prophet attacks the laws and practices because they fall short of what is required by the justice that transcends the laws and practices.

The prophets say very little about how to get from here to there—very little about how to get from the social injustices of one's present society to a society in which those injustices are removed. They do not pinpoint the laws that must be changed in their society, they do not mention the political activities that must take place to get those laws changed. They provide very little advice to social activists. If the ancient Israelites were like us, this

7   Social justice can also take the form of defending laws and public social practices that secure justice when those laws and practices are threatened.

silence on the part of the prophets would have been a source of annoyance to many. "If you're so smart and think you know everything that's wrong about America, why don't you tell us how to fix things and get down in the trenches and start fixing them, instead of just lobbing grenades over the wall? Talk is cheap."

The prophet does not see it as his calling to get into the nitty-gritty of legal and social reform. He's doing what has to be done first. He's trying to open the eyes of those with power so that they see the injustices they are perpetrating, trying to unstop their ears so that they hear the cries of those afflicted, trying to soften their hardened hearts so that they are moved.

Though the prophet does not give practical advice to reformers, what he does do, beyond launching his critique, is imagine a society in which things are different. He employs social imagination. Some of the most lyrically visionary passages in all of Western literature are expressions of the social imagination of the Hebrew prophets. The prophet imagines a day when the bonds of wickedness are loosed and the thongs of the yoke are undone, when the oppressed are let free and every yoke is broken, when people share their bread with the hungry, take the homeless poor into their houses, clothe the naked, and do not avert their eyes from their own kin (Isa. 58: 6–7).

By turning to the Hebrew prophets to understand the nature of social justice, I do not mean to suggest that opposition to social injustice must take the form of imitating the prophets. Often it should not. Often it should take the form of getting down into the trenches and trying to change things—trying to repeal the laws that oppress the weak and vulnerable, trying to replace those laws with laws that protect the weak and vulnerable, trying to get the government to enforce those laws, and so forth. And the rhetoric of those who speak up in opposition to social injustice need not always take the sharp accusatory form that it typically took in the prophets. Sometimes it should instead take the form of reasoning together.

Always, however, opposition to social injustice will have to aim at waking people up to what is happening, shaking them out of their slumber. And not infrequently that will require something other than reasoning together; not infrequently it will require sharp accusatory speeches, vivid presentations of the victims, and so forth. Much of the rhetoric of Martin Luther King, Jr. is an example of the point.

III

I said at the beginning of this essay that my topic is why so many people reject the idea of social justice. If social injustice is what I have suggested it is, namely, injustice perpetrated on members of society by laws and public social practices, and if social justice consists of speaking out against such injustice and doing what one reasonably can to undo it, then how could anybody be opposed to the idea of social justice? That's the question I want to address.

Some people are opposed to the idea of social justice because they are opposed to the idea of justice in general. They hold that we should be talking about people's responsibilities, not about their rights. Or that we should be talking about loving each other, not about doing what justice requires. Or, coming from the opposite end of the spectrum, that we should each ask what's in it for oneself and not busy ourselves with the rights of the other. On this occasion I want to set off to the side those who are opposed to the idea of justice in general and consider only those who don't like the idea of social justice in particular. Before I do that, however, let me describe for you the form I saw the objection to justice in general take on my first visit to South Africa.

It happened at a conference in Potchefstroom in 1975. Present at the conference were a sizable number of academics from South Africa—white, colored, and black, to use the categories employed at the time. Present were also people from other parts of Africa, a sizable contingent of people from the Netherlands, and a few of us from North America.

Apartheid was not the topic of the conference. Nonetheless, the Dutch exploited every opportunity they could find to express their opposition to apartheid, and the Afrikaners responded by exploiting every opportunity they could find to tell the Dutch in no uncertain terms that they were unfair, unloving, and morally arrogant. After a couple of days of this angry back-and-forth, the Dutch fell silent and the blacks and coloreds from South Africa began to speak up. They described the indignities daily heaped upon them, and they cried out for justice.

I was taken aback by the response of the Afrikaners to this cry. They insisted that justice was not a relevant category; benevolence was the relevant category. Apartheid was motivated by benevolence. There were some eleven different nationalities in South Africa. Apartheid was aimed at the great social good of enabling each of these nationalities to find its own unique identity. For that good to be achieved, these diverse nationalities had to be separated from each other. Hence, apartheid. It was unfortunate that attaining that great social good, of each nationality developing in its own unique way, required restricting the liberties of some people and creating misery in certain quarters. But it was all for the common good.

I saw, as I had never seen before, why the idea of social justice is indispensable. Justice applies the brakes to paternalistic benevolence. Social goods are not to be achieved at the cost of wronging people.

IV

One reason people are opposed to the idea of social justice is that they are turned off by the Mrs. Jellybys and the Miss Ansells of the world. Let me explain. Mrs. Jellyby is a character in Charles Dickens' novel *Bleak House*; she neglects her own children in order to devote all her time and energy to some great cause of social justice in Africa. "Miss Ansell" is the name of an actual Mrs. Jellyby with whom I had the ill fortune to become acquainted.

Miss Ansell owned a large Victorian house on the outskirts of Cambridge, England. In the fall of 1956 my wife and I rented two rooms on the second floor of her house; a young Israeli couple rented the other rooms on the floor. It became clear to us that they were very poor. This was at the time of the Hungarian Revolution. Miss Ansell spent all day every day at her desk writing letters to world figures urging them to do something to stop the Russian invasion of Hungary. She wrote to the British Prime Minister offering to lay her body across the tracks of the trains transporting Russian soldiers into Hungary if the British government would pay for the cost of her travel to Hungary.

Miss Ansell had a large garden back of her house, with a number of apple trees in it. The trees were ripe with fruit; the apples were beginning to fall. The Israeli couple asked if they could pick some of the apples. Miss Ansell tartly replied that they were not to go into the garden; the garden was off limits to her renters.

The eyes of Mrs. Jellyby were so firmly fixed on social injustices in distant Africa that she never saw that she was wronging her own children.

The eyes of Miss Ansell were so firmly fixed on injustice in distant Hungary that she never saw that she was wronging her renters. Such people give social justice a bad name. Their concern for social justice is combined with a mystifying and offensive oblivion or indifference to the injustice they are perpetrating at home. Not uncommonly they regard themselves as morally superior to those who are not similarly devoted to some great cause of social justice.

My response to those who oppose the idea of social justice because they are turned off by the Mrs. Jellybys and the Miss Ansells of the world is that they are right to be turned off by such people but not right to let that turn them against the idea of social justice itself. What we see in Mrs. Jellyby and Miss Ansell is a perversion of the moral life. Speaking up against and struggling against social injustice need not and should not come at the cost of being oblivious or indifferent to the injustices one is perpetrating at home.

Another reason people are opposed to the idea of social justice came up earlier in our discussion. Social justice requires being capable of a certain kind of pattern recognition; one has to look beyond particular episodes of injustice to discern regularities in these episodes. That done, one must then engage in a certain kind of social analysis; one must discern, as the cause of those regularities of injustice, laws and public social practices. And this latter discernment requires the ability to make a certain kind of abstraction; one must be able to abstract the laws, the practices, and their effects on victims from the attitudes toward the victims of those who institute or enforce the laws and of those who engage in the practices.

I mentioned that some people find this abstraction difficult. They don't think in terms of social practices; they are baffled by the charge that in acting as they do, they are perpetrating injustice. Others are not so much baffled as offended. How can their actions be tarred with perpetrating racial injustice when they don't have a racist bone in their bodies? How can their actions be tarred with wronging the poor when they give generously to the benevolence fund of their church or synagogue? They assume that to find out whether someone is perpetrating injustice, one looks to that person's intentions. Their own intentions are entirely good. They are good people. They contribute to charity. They teach Sunday School. They serve on vestry. They are members of the parish council.

This protest raises an important point—perhaps, for many, a surprising point. One's action can wrong someone, deprive her of what she has a right to, treat her unjustly, treat her with under-respect for her worth, without one's being blamable for performing that action. Perhaps one didn't know and couldn't be expected to know what one's action was doing to her. Or perhaps one did know but didn't realize and couldn't be expected to realize that one was treating her in a way that she had a right not to be treated. In each such case, one is not to be blamed but excused. Nonetheless it remains the case that one wronged her, treated her with under-respect. Injustice does not track with culpability; one can unwittingly wrong someone.

It is my impression that a good deal of resistance to the idea of social justice has its source in confusion on this point—confusion on both sides, both in the minds of those engaged in social justice and in the minds of those opposed to the idea of social justice. The person opposed to the idea of social justice assumes that if he concedes that some social practice in which he participates victimizes certain people, then he must also concede that he bears a burden of guilt. He insists that he does not bear a burden of guilt; his intentions have always been pure.

The thing to be said in response is that he may be right about that last point; it's possible that he does not bear a burden of guilt. But from the fact that he is not culpable it does not follow that he has not been wronging those affected by his actions. And let's not overlook the fact that his ignorance may be willful ignorance, in which case he is not to be excused.

A third reason people are opposed to the idea of social justice is that they hear the term "social justice" as a code word for the activities of those who favor an expansive welfare state. They have been led to believe that if they concede that the plight of the widows, the orphans, and the impoverished is not merely unfortunate but unjust, then they are committed to asking the state to dispense welfare to them or to introduce a large body of regulations. But they regard an expansive regulatory and welfare state as an all-enveloping octopus. So they oppose the idea of social justice.

The assumption is false. Recognizing that something is a social injustice carries no implications whatsoever as to how that injustice should be remedied; in particular, it does not carry the implication that the state is the remedy of first resort. No Hebrew prophet said that the remedy for the social injustice of poverty is that the king hand out doles to the poor.

The state should seldom be the remedy of first resort for undoing social injustice; it should almost always be the remedy of last resort. Far better if the practitioners of slavery had acknowledged its injustice and stopped the practice, rather than insisting on perpetuating the practice and forcing the state to intervene. Far better if our capitalist economy provided work and a living wage to all adults who can work, rather than failing to do so and forcing the state to intervene by dispensing welfare so that people won't starve. Far better if our market economy made it possible for everyone to afford health insurance, rather than falling far short of that and forcing the state to intervene by regulating the health insurance industry. And so forth.

The concept of imperfect rights that we introduced earlier is relevant here. An objection sometimes lodged against the idea of social justice is that it cannot be true that to be the victim of involuntary impoverishment is to have one's rights violated, since there is no one to whom one can point such that it is against *that* person that one has these rights. The argument is fallacious. One can have a right to be treated a certain way by someone or other without there being someone such that it is against *that* person that one has that right. The rights of the widows, the orphans, and the impoverished are, in good measure, imperfect rights.

V

My project in this essay has been to unearth and appraise the reasons people have for rejecting the idea of social justice. Some people reject the idea because they are put off by the Mrs. Jellybys and the Miss Ansells of the world. Others reject the idea because they find it either difficult or offensive to believe that good people like themselves could be guilty of inflicting injustice when they are simply doing business as business is done and contributing, out of the goodness of their hearts, to charitable organizations. Yet others reject the idea because they have been led to believe that to acknowledge something as a social injustice is to commit oneself to appealing to the state as the remedy of first resort, and they see this as leading to a state that is a menace to freedom.

Let me close by noting that another source of resistance to the idea of social injustice is that such resistance is often intertwined with rejection of the charge that one is a perpetrator of social injustice. One way of rejecting the charge is to question the moral standing of the person who has issued the negative moral judgment. Your judgment against me is arbitrary: why are you criticizing me for what I am doing when you say nothing about those people over there whose actions are just as bad or worse? Your judgment against me is hypocritical: why are you criticizing me for what I am doing when the practices in which you yourself are engaged are just as bad? Your judgment against me is morally arrogant: what makes you assume that you aren't just as morally blind as you think the rest of us are? Another way of rejecting the charge that one is a perpetrator of social injustice is to agree that the plight of the purported victims is indeed unfortunate but then go on to insist that it's their own fault, so it's not a case of injustice, or that there's nothing to be done about it that won't make matters worse, so it's not a case of injustice.

Acknowledging that one is complicit in social injustice requires that one commit oneself to desist from the practice or reform it, if either of those is possible; and often that's more than a person can bring himself to do. One would make much less money, lose esteem among friends, no longer be in a position of privilege and power. That's too high a price. Best to keep one's position of privilege, power, and pelf, fend off the charge of injustice in one way or another, and make generous contributions to charitable organizations. Not justice but charity: that's the way to go. Then nothing has to change. The reason social justice movements are almost always conflictual is that those who benefit from the status quo find the price of change too high.

VI

Consider the great social justice movements of the past century and a half: the abolitionist movement was a social justice movement, the movement for the control of monopolies was a social justice movement, the campaign for the abolition of child labor was a social justice movement, the labor union movement was a social justice movement, the campaign for women's rights was a social justice movement, the passage of Social Security legislation was the result of a social justice movement, the civil rights movement was a social justice movement. The list goes on and on. How different our society would be if none of these movements for social justice had occurred. Though all justice is social, not all justice is social justice. Social justice is, however, an enormously important part of the whole.

Chapter Three
Social Justice Isn't What You Think It Is

Michael Novak
American Enterprise Institute and Ave Maria University

In this chapter, I will begin by asking what most people think social justice is, noting five different ways the term is used. After that, I will turn to the question of how the term arose—arguing that it is a Catholic concept, later taken over (and transformed) by secular progressives. What social justice actually is turns out to be very different from the way the term is now used popularly.

When the Academics Take Over: Five Common Usages of Social Justice

Distribution

Most people's sense of social justice is generic, amounting to nothing more than what we find in the dictionary under "social justice": "The distribution of advantages and disadvantages in society." Now, notice that the dictionary definition introduces a new key term, "distribution." Alas, the original notion of social justice had very little to do with distribution. Worse, this newly added term suggests that some extra-human force, "the visible hand," does the distribution, that is, some very powerful human agency (usually the State).

Equality

Furthermore, the expression "advantages and disadvantages" supposes there is a norm of "equality" by which to measure "disadvantages." Consider this professorial definition: although it is difficult to agree on the precise meaning of "social justice," I take that, to most of us, it implies, among other things, equality of the burdens, the advantages, and the opportunities of citizenship. Indeed, I take that social justice is intimately related to the concept of equality, and that the violation of it is intimately related to the concept of inequality.

This definition expresses a whole ideology—one that is simply assumed rather than explained and defended—that "equality" is good and ought to be enforced. And note what has happened to the word "equality." In English, equality often does not mean "literally the same" but rather suggests fairness, equity, or the equitable. What is equitable is often not to give people the same portions, but rather to give what is proportionate to the efforts of each. But in European languages, most thinkers followed the model of the French term *égalité*. *Égalité* means the "equals sign," *égal*. "This" on one side is equal to "that" on the other side. *Égalité* is a quite different notion from the English "equitable." This French/Continental usage is captured in the *American Sociological Review*:

> As I see it, social justice requires resource equity, fairness, and respect for diversity, as well as the eradication of existing forms of social oppression. Social justice entails a "redistribution" of resources from those who have "unjustly" gained them to those who justly deserve them, and it also means creating and "ensuring" the processes of truly democratic participation in decision-making. . . . It seems clear that only a "decisive" redistribution of resources and decision-making power can "ensure" social justice and authentic democracy.[1]

In brief, shifting to the French *égalité* changes the entire meaning of equality from equity or fairness to arithmetical uniformity. This is really a dreadful change, because where people take equality very seriously, they soon insist on uniformity. In the Inca society under Spanish rule, the first utopia was attempted; people were assigned by social class certain colors

---

1   Joe R. Feagin, "Social Justice and Sociology: Agendas for the Twenty-First Century," Presidential Address, *American Sociological Review*, Vol. 66, No. 1 (February 2001).

of robes to wear, and regimented hours were established for everything that was to be done throughout the day—even lovemaking hours, with great emphasis on bringing forth more children. If you are going to make everybody equal, you really have to make uniform crucial items of daily life.

Common Good

Social justice is typically associated with some notion of the "common good." "Common good" is a wonderful term that goes back to Aristotle. But in practice, it often hinges on a key question, namely, who decides "What is the common good?" In ancient societies, often the wisest and strongest person was the ruler, and it was he who made the important decisions, such as where we will camp tonight, or near which source of water we shall build our village. The person with the greatest strategic and tactical sense of what is safe, and the greatest ecological sense of where there will be good community life, would make these decisions.

But in contemporary times, beginning a century or two ago, that responsibility gradually shifted to the bureaucratic state. Decisions became too numerous for the ruler himself to make, and they were delegated to a variety of organizations. Further, such decisions came to be decided by many people at once. No longer is there one clear person to be held responsible and accountable for these decisions. Quickly, the beautiful notion of the common good gets ensnared in red tape.

A central misuse of the term common good became clear to me for the first time when, at the Human Rights Commission in Bern, I was prodding the Soviet delegation to recognize the right of married couples, one of whose partners was from one nation, the other from another, to share residence in whichever nation they chose. The Soviets staunchly resisted—in the name of the common good. The Soviet Union, they insisted, had invested great sums of money and much effort in giving an education to each Soviet citizen. The common good, they said, demands that these citizens now make comparable contributions in return. Therefore, the Soviet partner could not leave. Individual desires must bow to the (supposed) common good of all.

In this way, the common good becomes an excuse for total state control—an excuse on which totalitarianism was built. You can achieve the common good better if there is a total authority, and you must then subordinate the desires and wishes of individuals to a vast, impersonal bureaucratic state.

As a result, there are many occasions when one must argue for individual rights against arguments made in the name of the common good. Most people rightly understand the concept of the "common good" to be something noble and good, a commitment to the true well-being of all citizens. But often those who have the power to decide what the common good is and enforce those decisions abuse the power terribly. So a ritual invocation of the "common good" can hardly provide an adequate conception of social justice.

The Progressive Agenda

Social justice is often simply identified with a Progressive agenda. To begin with, then, we need to understand the background of progressivism. The Progressive agenda began as a critical response to the new discoveries and the new vitalities introduced by what would soon become known as capitalism. Beginning in about 1600, European societies began experiencing a turbulent, dramatic shift from agrarian society to crowded commercial towns. The first craftsmen of Italy and France and Germany set up their workshops in towns and small cities (which kept growing). They didn't live on the farms or make their living from the land. They made their living from their wit, from their crafts, from their skills, and they usually had to work together. They were known as town-dwellers (those who live in towns), and they became the first "bourgeoisie."

Of course, today "bourgeois" has become a pejorative term. If you were told, "You have such bourgeois taste," you might be uncertain what that meant, but you knew it wasn't meant as a compliment. But should that be the case? If you think about it, many of the people of best taste in the world have been the bourgeoisie. Who makes the best wines, the best cheeses, the best lace and millinery? Who makes the best cutlery, or fashions the best wooden tables? Many of the beautiful things of Europe have been made by the bourgeoisie. In their little ateliers, even the painters had their schools, their little factories for paintings, if you wish, in which apprentices would fill in the background work which the master would finish. Thus painters in the nineteenth century—in fact, from the sixteenth century on—often created in workshops, not as isolated individuals. And they congregated in cities, because that is where they would have to come to learn these skills, and that is where the market for portraits was.

From Horace and Virgil on, there have been those who didn't like the world created by the bourgeoisie. Such poets of pastoral life preferred to think that farming and fishing are more "natural"—what God gave us to do. They were hostile to the "middlemen," who buy their produce or fish and transport them and sell them, who "buy cheap and sell dear," in a way they considered unfair. For centuries, there has been a widespread attack on the bourgeoisie and the unfairness and inequity of a commercial system, especially among artists and intellectuals, who consider their work to be superior to commercial work and often resent the higher monetary returns merchants or businessmen receive for their work.

The early stages of progressivism focused especially on labor. As the number and the range of these little workshops increased, moving from perhaps ten to maybe fifty workers, the factory system began to grow. Now for the first time, working people were cut off from their farms, so they no longer grew their own food. They worked long hours in the factory, just as they worked long hours in the country—for neither in the country nor in the factories did they work only eight-hour days. Just as they worked from sunup until sunset in the country, so they did in the cities and in the factories too. (There is sometimes a modern tendency to wax nostalgic about "country living" and "working in the fresh air," forgetting that it was very difficult, almost unending work that was painfully vulnerable to the vagaries of nature.)

One potential problem in the growing cities and expanding factories was that workers were now entirely dependent on their wages—that is, on those who paid them. In the past, on farms, those who had a roof over their heads and enough to eat weren't destitute (barring natural disasters, such as droughts and famines). But in the new towns and cities where workers became wage-dependent, some writers now spoke of "wage slavery," because the workers became so dependent on their employers that they lost their rural independence. Moreover, they often lost the solidity of their former, deeply-rooted way of life, with its extensive kinship networks and religious framework (such as the yearly liturgical seasons).

In the face of these new circumstances—often a loss of social ties and a shared way of life, combined with entire dependence on an employer for the wages to guarantee their subsistence—the Progressive agenda was to "right" some of the wrongs to which these new workers might be subject, especially harsh or arbitrary treatment by their employers. It meant being on the side of labor, the proletariat,[2] as Marx put it.

But, if labor was for a long time its central focus, the post-1960s era saw a dramatic transformation of the Progressive agenda. While "labor" was still an important element, other "disadvantaged groups" emerged as central concerns. Racial minorities were central to the civil rights revolution, which deeply shaped 1960s progressives and helped create wide public sympathy for reform. It became a "template" for other "liberation" movements, especially the liberation of women from past limitations and stereotypes.

Ironically, the expansion of women's rights—much of which is uncontroversial today—led to a curious contraction of the progressivist impulse to expand protections to new groups. In the interest of giving women control over their childbearing, progressives embraced a new agenda of "Reproductive Rights." As one writer puts it,

> The privileged in this world, for the most part, have unfettered access to the reproductive health and education services to decide for themselves when and whether to bear or raise a child. The poor and disadvantaged do not. Thus, the struggle for reproductive justice is inextricably bound up with the effort to secure a more just society.
>
> Accordingly, those who would labor to achieve economic and social justice are called upon to join in the effort to achieve

---

2 "Proletariat" is a word invented to mean people who work in factories, something that Marx and others thought hadn't existed before. It's worth noting, however, that in fifteenth-century Venice there was a huge factory for making cannon, the best cannon in the world, and in Spain there were other factories making cannon that some people thought were even better. Some scholars even argue that during the 500-year sea war between the Muslims and the Christians, the Venetian and Spanish cannon tipped the balance, until even the Muslims conceded the point and began to bribe engineers and others, pay them very well, and bring them to Byzantium or Turkey to open operations there. So there were already factories in earlier ages. Interestingly—contrary to Max Weber—these most often grew up in Catholic countries first.

reproductive justice and, thereby, help realize the sacred vision of a truly just society for all.[3]

That "decision for themselves when and whether to bear or raise a child" was taken by progressives to mean that women must have the legal right to abort children they had conceived. "Social justice" now meant the right of one formerly disadvantaged group to eliminate members of another group (unborn children) that are sometimes considered obstacles to their own well-being.

More recently, the progressive agenda has expanded to the case of gay rights. Consider the following:

> How can the [Anglican] Church be taken seriously or receive any respect for its views on the far more important issues of poverty, violence and social justice when the public keep being reminded of this blot on its integrity, the continued discrimination against gays?[4]

The new focus on gay rights, however, meant that the social institution of marriage had to be bent to its demands. The social interest in marriage—above all, the interest in bearing and educating the next generation of citizens—was subordinated to the imperative of expanding equality.

So, unsurprisingly, it turns out that "social justice" is identified with the current focus of the Progressive agenda.

Compassion

One final lens through which social justice is viewed is "compassion." There used to be a Tammany Hall saying: "Th' fella' w'at said that patriotism is the last refuge of scoundrels, underestimated th' possibilities of compassion." In addition to equality and the common good, a third term that

---

3   Clergymen for Reproductive Justice, quoted in "A Catholic College and Abortion Advocates—Here We Go Again," *Catholic Online*, 2009. (www.catholic.org/news/hf/faith/story.php?id=33617).

4   Russell Armitage, quoted in "Gay Minister Claims Discrimination," *Stuff*, 2009 (www.stuff.co.nz/510018/Gay-minister-claims-discrimination).

came to be closely associated with social justice was compassion. One of the most extraordinary political developments since about 1832 is that everything is done in the name of the poor. Modern "revolutions" are almost all fought in the name of the poor (not in the United States, but in the rest of the world), though the track record of "revolutionary systems" in helping the poor is spotty at best.

The Tammany Hall saying wittily calls attention to the fact that more sins—an extraordinary number of murders—have been committed in the name of compassion in the last 150 years—by the Nazis, by the Communists, and by the African and Asian despots who justify their regimes as "socialist"—than by any other force in history. We must not allow that beautiful term "compassion" to blind us. There are true forms and false forms.

In an entirely different order of magnitude, why did the Progressive impulse toward "compassion" during the "War on Poverty" (1964 and thereafter) have the effect of destroying so many families? Over a third of the pregnancies in Washington, D.C., end in abortion. And then of those who are born, 70 percent are born outside of wedlock. What is happening in this country is the largest-scale abandonment of women by men in human history. And not only in urban areas; it's happening out in Iowa, Ohio, and all across the country. (Charles Murray wrote a famous article on out-of-wedlock births in Ohio.) Such births are now multiplying throughout the developed countries; they are appearing more in countries like Italy, France, Germany, and in Great Britain (where almost half of all births are out-of-wedlock).

This chain of events was unleashed in the name of a war against poverty, a war to reduce crime, a war to help the family. But if you look at what actually happened, that war on poverty has not been an unmixed blessing. It worked very well for the elderly; the condition of the elderly in the United States since 1965, let's say, is far better. In fact, if anything, the elderly get too much, and now we're having great problems with the commitments we made for Medicare and even our inability to keep funding the promised Social Security. The premise of Social Security arrangements was that there would be seven workers for every benefit receiver. Today, however, we are no longer having the required numbers of children. We're getting to the point where there are about two workers for every retiree. It is therefore already clear that we are not going to be able to meet the obligations that we have assumed. That sword of Damocles hangs by an even more frayed thread in Europe. There is going to be a great crisis of social democracy in the next ten years.

This survey suggests that "social justice" has no very clear meaning today, and often it is little more than a code word for advancing particular political agendas. Let me finish with an anecdote: I recently read the obituary of a Franciscan sister, out in Delaware, who had worked as a missionary in different countries. The author described her as being especially committed to "social justice work." She helped feed the hungry, tend to the young, care for the ill. She labored for the neediest. In this usage, "social justice" seems rather like a synonym for "following the Beatitudes." That work was certainly admirable, but usage like this gives us very little conceptual content for "social justice."

What Did Social Justice Originally Mean?

Taparelli—Modern Problems Call for a New Virtue

Now, I would like to consider the way the term "social justice" originally emerged in modern history. Where did it come from? The first known usage of the term is by an Italian priest, Luigi Taparelli D'Azeglio, who wrote a book about the need for recovering the ancient virtue of what had been called "general justice" in Aristotle and Thomas Aquinas, but in a new contemporary form. He gave it the term "social justice."

Taparelli wasn't clear what he was looking for, but he was clear about the problems, some of which I've outlined above: the movement away from the country to the cities, moving away from the family food supply, becoming wage-dependent, family members going to work in different locations. The strain on the family was enormous.

Leo XIII, Rerum Novarum (1891)—The Evil of Equality

Pope Leo XIII became the first of the modern popes to really use encyclicals (a letter to the whole world) as means of communication. Up until the eighteenth century, Christianity was primarily in Europe, with smaller missionary centers generally ruled from Europe in other parts of the world. By 1890, that was increasingly not the case, as thriving societies emerged in North and South America, and there were more and more organized dioceses and parishes all around the world. Encyclicals became an important means to communicate with the various parts of this worldwide Church.

One of the most important of these encyclicals Leo XIII entitled *Rerum novarum*, meaning "the new things," the "new times." What he meant were the things I have been describing, especially the move from farms to urban areas and especially the resultant strain on families.

Some people ask, "What is a pope doing, writing about economic and social matters? That's not a pope's province." But the cradle of Catholicism—of Christianity more generally—has always been the family. That's where children first learn, by the look in their mother's eyes when she holds them, and the warmth of being held, the meaning of unconditional love and of concern for someone beyond self—elementary human experiences that prepare them for Christianity. And then that initial understanding is further nourished in many different ways in the family, providing a foundation for the practice of the Christian faith. The crisis of the family—already in 1890—was something the pope knew needed to be addressed. He wanted to call attention to the fact that societies were now being organized on principles entirely different from the whole preceding history of Christianity. Earlier, almost all Christians—like everyone else—had been farmers, or associated with farming. If you read the New Testament, you see that quite vividly, for example, in the parables of the good shepherd and the sower of the seed; indeed, almost all of the parables are agrarian in background. But more and more people were not living agrarian lives, and Leo XIII had to confront the question of Christianity's response to these new circumstances.

Let me point out one particularly important passage from *Rerum novarum* that deals with the question of social equality. The background to this passage is the threat the pope sees in socialism, the theory of giving the state total power. (He doesn't use the term "totalitarian," but he might have.) Very early in the encyclical he discusses "civil society." For Leo, civil society is a good term; "civil" comes from the Latin for the town, the city, the citizen. It gains its force from the experience of the medieval towns, centers of safety, commerce, craftsmanship, and prosperity—generally, the centers of the highest prosperity and the greatest freedom. Max Weber even wrote: "City air breathes free." When you come to the towns, you're free. That's where the universities are, that's where the new commerce is, and that's where people come from far and near to examine the goods that came from many regions, and to set up trading arrangements. What is the relationship of civil society to equality?

Here is Leo XIII's attack on the very ideal of equality as a social ideal:

> Therefore, let it be laid down in the first place that in civil society, the lowest cannot be made equal with the highest. Socialists, of course, agitate to the contrary, but all struggling against nature is in vain. There are truly very great and very many natural differences among men. Neither the talents nor the skill nor the health nor the capacities of all are the same, and unequal fortune follows of itself upon necessary inequality in respect to these endowments.[5]

These words are in one of the older translations of the encyclical. Here is the more modern translation on the Vatican website:

> It must be first of all recognized that the condition of things inherent in human affairs must be borne with, for it is impossible to reduce civil society to one dead level. Socialists may in that intent do their utmost, but all striving against nature is in vain. There naturally exist among mankind manifold differences of the most important kind; people differ in capacity, skill, health, strength; and unequal fortune is a necessary result of unequal condition.[6]

It's really a rather simple, but very important, observation. The pope goes on to say:

> Such inequality is far from being disadvantageous either to individuals or to the community. Social and public life can only

---

5   *Rerum novarum*, no. 26.
6   *Rerum novarum*, no. 17 (w2.vatican.va/content/leo-xiii/en/encyclicals/documents/hf_l-xiii_enc_15051891_rerum-novarum.html).

be maintained by means of various kinds of capacity for business and the playing of many parts; and each man, as a rule, chooses the part which suits his own peculiar domestic condition.[7]

The fact that we're unequal is a benefit—"for to carry on its affairs, community life requires varied aptitudes and diverse services. And to perform these diverse services, men are impelled most by differences in individual property holdings." This becomes his defense of the crucial role of the ownership of private property for incarnate beings like ourselves. If we were angels, we wouldn't need property. But if a human being is going to be free, he has to own "his own stuff," he has to have a place to which he can repair that somebody can't take away from him.

Thus Leo XIII did not mean by "social justice" equality. On the contrary, Leo held that it's good that there's an unequal society. Different people are fitted for different kinds of work, and it's wonderful to be able to find the work that fits your talents. This had been an argument that the founders of the United States used to justify a commercial system, that it provided more opportunities for a wider range of skills than farming life did, and so it allowed a much larger range of talents to mature and to develop as people found different niches for themselves.

Rerum novarum, then, addresses the evil of equality. Equality is against nature and undermines the development of the whole range of human gifts. Human gifts make us necessarily unequal, in some sense. Naturally, God is not impressed by the talents of any human being. No matter how great anybody's talents are, they don't come anywhere close to God, who created all beauty and all power and all energy and all ability. In that sense, in the eyes of God, we're all equal. Relative to God, the differences between us aren't important in the way God sees us. But in terms of looking at each of us realistically in our social roles, we are very different, and that's what makes society work. Not everybody has to be slotted to be a cog in a machine.

Nothing demonstrates this diversity in individuals better than the difference between raising children and training animals. It's easier to bring up cats than children. My two daughters each brought home a stray kitten

---

7   *Rerum novarum*, no. 17.

that they promised to take care of—we parents would never have to take care of them. Then they graduated from high school, they went away to college, they left home, and we inherited the damn cats. We didn't know how to train them very well at first (disciplining their instincts), so they developed very bad habits . . . Bringing up children, however, is a very different task: you have to prepare them to be free, to be responsible.

Children cannot be merely "trained," because they have multiple sets of warring instincts, and they themselves have to learn how to balance these warring passions—recognize them, become master of them, learn self-control—to become free. That's what freedom is.

That freedom is at the heart of human individuality and diversity—which is such an important part of society, and from which it benefits so greatly. That's why Pope Leo was so dead set against the idea of equality understood as sameness. He wanted, rather, to praise the diversity of human gifts and human vocations and human callings.

A New Virtue of Association

Now, what the pope was reaching for in *Rerum novarum* was the same thing Taparelli introduced—namely, that under the new circumstances the world was confronting, there was a need for Christians to develop new habits, new virtues. He didn't know the name for this new virtue, but he was groping for it. If you don't want the State to run everything, what are you going to need? You're going to need people who are able to cooperate and associate among themselves, to solve problems on their own level—at the level of civil society—by themselves. If you want a playground for your children, you've got to cooperate with others in the neighborhood to build it. If you want to keep its equipment up, you've got to cooperate to paint it. If your village well is inefficient, you've got to organize together to dig a deeper one.

So the pope was trying to identify something that would engender the spirit and the practice of association. In fact, he came to be known as the "Pope of Association." He understood that this was actually a great inheritance from the Middle Ages. For example, in the towns one group would adopt a bridge and would be responsible for its upkeep, and they'd be allowed to collect a toll to pay for the necessary repairs. Others would adopt roads, and so forth. Associations took responsibility for the different needs of life in the village and the town. If you go through Europe today, especially in Italy, you still see these sorts of associations. Each member sometimes wears a different colored ribbon or special flag to identify himself as a member of that association.

So in the second half of the nineteenth century, more and more of the laity were sharing a transition such as my grandparents experienced in the little country of Slovakia in the center of Europe. My grandparents' central civic and Christian duties for centuries had been simple: to pray, pay, and obey. If they did those three things, they were good humans and good Christians. But when their children moved to America, many different responsibilities were imposed upon them. They were no longer subjects of the emperor but citizens of a free republic—sovereign in their power. If something was wrong and needed fixing, they were obliged to organize with others to fix it. They organized their own insurance companies to take care of families with men who were hurt in the mill or the mine. They organized their own clubs, and they organized their own recreation; the Slovak Sokol "falcon" is the symbol for athletics. Lots of beer was served and the men, even the old men, used to show up at the Sokol to play board games. Meanwhile, the young people would train to march, dance, and sing in yearly festivals. The different ethnic groups did this in different ways, but they all did it, through the life of association.

So, there's a new possibility in the new world. More and more people are getting educated. More and more are living independent of the land; more and more are getting used to a life of association and working with others. That is precisely what the pope encouraged in *Rerum novarum*. If we don't understand the importance of association, we have no answer for socialism. You can't answer statism unless you have an alternative. The pope didn't use the term statism then, but I think that's a reasonable name for what we are facing today, because today the State is the rapidly growing leviathan.

If the State has all the responsibilities, it gains all the power, with predictably terrible consequences. In *Rerum novarum*, Leo XIII predicted nine different things that would happen under socialism, and they all did, if you look at it from the perspective of 1989, after the fall of the Wall (as I know many people in Central Europe did). Everything he predicted from the drive for equality came true: the forced uniformity, the killing of creativity and originality, and, ultimately, the breakdown of the whole system. In the socialist system, there was practically no new source of wealth, no invention of products for world market (except the splendid Kalashnikov). If the Soviets wanted a new technology or a new tool, they had to steal it, and they became very good at that. But they were always a generation or two behind.

The last point I shall make is something that Friedrich Hayek wrote about in a really powerful little book called *The Mirage of Social Justice*,[8] in which he picked up on the way the term "social justice" was being used in the first half of the twentieth century. He said "social justice" had become a synonym for "progressive," and "progressive" in practice meant socialist or heading toward socialism. Hayek well understood the Catholic lineage of social justice, how the term had first appeared in Catholic thought, and then the subsequent development, until almost 100 years later it became dominant on the secular Left. The popes, Hayek noted, had described social justice as a virtue. Now, a virtue is a habit, a set of skills. Imagine a simple set of skills, such as driving a car. The social habit of association and cooperation for attending to public needs is an important, newly learned habit widely practiced, especially in America. Social justice is learning how to form small "bands of brothers" outside the family who, for certain purposes, volunteer to give time and effort to accomplish something. If there are many children who aren't learning how to read, you volunteer for tutoring.

Tocqueville said a most fascinating and insightful thing about America, namely, that wherever in France people turned to *l'Etat*, and wherever in Britain people turned to the aristocracy, in America people got together and formed associations.[9] They held bake sales to send missionaries to the Antipodes, to build colleges. They invented a hundred devices to raise money among themselves. That's what a free people does. That's what a democracy is. The first law of democracy, Tocqueville wrote, is the law of association. If you want to free people, so that they are not swallowed up by the State, you have to develop in them the virtue of cooperation and association. It's not an easy virtue to learn at first, but it soon becomes a vast

8   Hayek, F. A. *Law, Legislation, and Liberty, Volume 2: The Mirage of Social Justice* (Chicago: University of Chicago Press), 1978.

9   Alexis de Tocqueville, *Democracy in America*, Vol. II, Part II, chapter 5.

social phenomenon. It's not at all uncommon for thirty college students to show up for a presidential campaign in, say, New Hampshire and organize the whole state for their candidate. They've never done that before, but they know how to use a rolodex, and they can very soon organize an entire state. It's a skill they learned. It's one of the great skills of Americans.

In America, it sometimes seems that we mostly go to meetings. Parenthood, you discover, is essentially a transportation service. Your kids go to so many meetings in a day you need a sign on the refrigerator telling you which times everybody is scheduled for what, and where they have to be. Americans are good at going to meetings, and that's a tremendous skill to have. You can send a group of Americans in the Peace Corps, even a dozen of them, and they'll figure out what they need to do and organize themselves to do it. You don't have to write detailed orders from headquarters.

And that's what, in a word, social justice is—a virtue, a habit that people internalize and learn, a capacity. It's a capacity that has two sides: first, a capacity to organize with others to accomplish particular ends, and secondly, the ends that you want to accomplish are extra-familial. They're for the good of the neighborhood, or the village, or the town, or the state, or the country, or the world. To send money or clothes or to travel to other parts of the world in order to help out. That's what social justice is. Part of the new order of the ages, "rerum novarum."

Finally, it's important to note that this notion of social justice is ideologically neutral. It is as common to people on the Left to organize and form associations, to cooperate in many social projects, as it is to people on the Right. This is not a loaded political definition, but it does avoid the pitfall (common on the Left) of thinking that social justice means distribution, égalité, the common good only as determined by State authority, and so forth. It also avoids the pitfall (on the Right) of thinking of the individual as unencumbered, closed-up, self-contained, self-sufficient.

It is, therefore, no accident that the virtue of social justice slumbered for so many centuries, until the profound disruption of social conditions and a new set of civil institutions called it into life and new prominence.

Chapter Four

On the Origins of the Concept of Social Justice and a Misunderstanding of Aquinas

John Finnis

Oxford University and

University of Notre Dame Law School

The term "social justice" was introduced into the magisterial teaching of the Catholic Church in Pius XI's encyclical *Quadragesimo anno* (1931), having entered French, Italian,[1] and English discourse, with something like its elusive modern meaning, in the half-century after 1830. The term's use in the encyclical can help us grasp a main part, at least, of its useful meaning. Section 57 (in the numbering now conventional) says that "the law of social justice" is "that the common good of all society be kept inviolate."[2] And it articulates this principle in the context of the institution of property: that institution is for a purpose, the common good (or advantage) of all, and not every distribution of private property rights is compatible with that

---

1 On French and Italian origins, see Pierre Vallin, "Aux origines de l'expression 'Justice Sociale'," *Chronique Sociale de France* 68 (1960), 379–92. See also Alfred Fouillée, "L'Idée de justice sociale d'après les écoles contemporaines," *Revue de Deux Mondes* 59 (1899), t. 152, 47–75 (unlike the individualist justice of Herbert Spencer, "la justice sociale protégé au besoin le faible contre le fort, tient compte du passé et songe d'avenir": p. 52); Paulin Malapert, "La Justice sociale" in *Questions de morale* (Alcan, Paris, 1900), 286–310; M. S. Gillet, *Conscience chrétienne et justice sociale* (Paris, 1922), 134ff; Gillet, "Le Problème social et la justice sociale," *Revue de Philosophie* 26 (1926), 156–88, 267–77.

2 Similarly, sec. 110 says that the "norm of social justice" is "the needs of the common good."

purpose. Claims that the sole title to ownership is labor are as contrary to social justice as claims by the wealthy to retain all the fruits of their ownership without distributing any of it to workers.[3] Again (sec. 71), "social justice demands that changes be introduced as soon as possible whereby every adult workingman will be assured of a wage large enough to meet ordinary family needs adequately." For "it is an intolerable abuse, to be abolished at all costs, that mothers are forced, on account of the father's low wage, to engage in gainful employment outside the home to the neglect of their proper cares and responsibilities, especially the training of children." More generally, social justice demands (sec. 74) that wages be "so managed by agreement of plans and wills" that they are set neither too high (causing unemployment and consequent social disorder) nor too low to provide adequate means of livelihood, measured by the needs of a family. And looking at the economic system as a whole, the encyclical says (sec. 88) that both "social justice and social charity" call for the control of the dictatorship of monopolies and cartels that displaces free competition—a competition which itself needs to be kept within certain limits by public authority guided by social charity. Capital (the class of owners) violates social justice (and the common good, and the dignity of workers) when it controls the non-owning working class, and the whole economic system, to its own will and advantage (sec. 101).

What is common to these uses of the term "social justice" is that they concern, not—or not directly and primarily—the distribution of some common stock, but the impact and side effects of relationships which are (at least primarily) between private individuals or entities, such as relationships of employment, or the use to which owners put that part of their property that exceeds their needs (however broadly conceived). In this way, the encyclical's use of "social justice" matches the term's early usage in English, notably John Stuart Mill's reference, on the penultimate page of his

---

3   Sec. 110 will say that relations between capital or ownership and work or labor "must be made to conform to the laws of strictest justice—commutative justice, as it is called." This is not spelled out, but is a matter of the equality of exchange, i.e., of the value being given and received on each side of a contract, e.g., of employment (sale, as it were, of work): see Finnis, *Aquinas: Moral, Political and Legal Theory* (OUP, 1998), 200–203.

Utilitarianism (1861), to "the highest abstract standard of social and distrib-utive justice." For although the context of Mill's phrase—the ambitious and incipiently socialist claim that "society should treat all equally well who have deserved equally well of it"—is far removed from the encyclical's, we can ask why Mill added "social" to "distributive." And the answer to that question, we may reasonably infer from the body of Mill's contemporaneous writings, is that although some governmental responsibilities and powers, such as taxation, are directly matters of distributive justice (distributing, in this case, burdens according to fair shares), others relate to incidents or side effects of relationships and activities that are private, such as contract-ing and bequeathing, which government and law regulate, without at all managerially controlling, in the interests of fair equality.[4] To cover this as-pect of Mill's ideal of equality (an ideal which this is not the place to con-sider), he feels, we may speculate, the need for a qualification or specification of justice to supplement the qualifier "distributive."

Pius XI, unlike Mill, was working within a long and well-articulated tradition of thought about justice. Why, then, did he and his advisers feel the need to reach beyond the well-established Aristotelian, Thomist, and Neo-Scholastic categories, "distributive" and "commutative" justice, and introduce to the tradition a term unknown to it: "social justice"? The answer given by Giorgio del Vecchio in 1946 seems correct, and was followed and supplemented in my *Natural Law and Natural Rights*.[5] It is not too late to summarize it with further refinements still.

In line with the structure of the first parts of Book V of Aristotle's *Nicomachean Ethics*, Aquinas holds that there is justice in general, a genus of virtue which has two species of "particular justice": distributive justice and commutative justice. The genus or "general virtue"[6] he usually calls

---

4   See, e.g., Huei Chun Su, "Is social justice for or against liberty? The philoso-phical foundations of Mill and Hayek's theory of liberty," *Review of Austrian Economics* 22 (2009) 387–414.

5   Giorgio del Vecchio, *La Giustizia* (3d ed., revised and enlarged) (Editrice Stu-dium, Rome, 1946), trans. A. H. Campbell, *Justice: an historical and philosophical essay* (Edinburgh University Press, 1952), 35–39; Finnis, *Natural Law and Na-tural Rights* (OUP, 1980, 2011), 164–65, 184–88, 196–97.

6   He explains (*Summa Theologiae* [*ST*] II–II q. 58 a. 6c) that this virtue is special, inasmuch as it is not essentially identical to virtue in general (that is, to all

"legal justice," because this virtue is concerned with bringing one's life into line with *common* good, and the criterion to be followed in settling what is for the common good is law, natural or positive.[7] It might have been better had he called it "general justice." Be that as it may, Aquinas poses and answers an objection: if commutative justice concerns appropriateness in dealings between individuals, and distributive justice appropriateness in sharing out of some common stock of benefits or burdens, shouldn't the latter (distributive) species of particular justice be regarded as a matter of legal justice (for the virtue he names legal justice is precisely about common matters)? To which Aquinas responds: distributive justice is about sharing out common stock to particular persons, whereas legal justice concerns directing to common good things/matters that belong or pertain to private persons [*ordinare ea quae sunt privatarum personarum in bonum commune*].[8] This response should put us in mind of the matters that Pius XI concretely talked about under the heading of social justice: the wages settled between employers and employees, the disposition by rich people of their own wealth, the unrestrained dominance ("dictatorship") of a particular concern or enterprise in some market.

As we have seen, Aquinas made this response in the context of upholding the thesis that there are only *two* species of particular justice: commutative and distributive. Legal justice, in orienting private matters to common good, is not another particular kind of justice, he thinks; justice, after all, is all about orienting us to common good. But his great early-sixteenth-century commentator, Thomas de Vio, Cardinal Cajetan, thought otherwise:

> There are three species of justice, as there are three types of relationships in any "whole": the relations of the parts amongst themselves, the relations of the whole to the parts, and the

---

the virtues, some of which are fundamentally about one's governance of oneself), but general inasmuch as it is concerned (a. 5c) with ensuring that one's self-governance is at least compatible with, and in due measure actually promotes, the common good of the various communities to which one belongs.

7   *ST* II–II q. 58 a. 5c.
8   *ST* II–II q. 61 a. 1 obj. 1 and ad 1.

relations of the parts to the whole. And likewise there are three justices: legal, distributive and commutative. For legal justice orients the parts to the whole, distributive the whole to the parts, while commutative orients the parts one to another.[9]

In a very short time, certainly by the time of Dominic Soto's treatise *De Justitia et Jure* (1556), the inner logic of Cajetan's synthesis was being worked out. A modern representative of the post-Cajetan tradition, writing as it happens within a year or two of *Quadragesimo anno*, puts it thus:

> Three kinds of order are required [by justice]: order of parts to whole, order of whole to parts, and order of one part to another. Legal justice pertains to the first sort, since it *governs the relationship of subjects to the State*. Distributive justice pertains to the second sort, since it governs the relationship of the State to its subjects. Commutative justice pertains to the third, governing the relationship of one private person or entity to another.[10]

Cajetan's triadic or triangular schema related Whole to Parts, Parts to Parts, and Parts to Whole. The subsequent Neo-Scholastic tradition summed up by Merkelbach had as the three sides of its similar triangle: State to Citizen, Citizen to Citizen, and Citizen (Subject) to State (Government). Legal justice is now little more than the subject/citizen's duty of allegiance to the state and its government and laws.

This schema is a misunderstanding of Aquinas. What Cajetan and those who followed him did not sufficiently notice, it seems, is not only Aquinas' refusal to treat legal justice as on the same level as—another species alongside—distributive and commutative justice but also his thesis

9   Cajetan (Thomas de Vio), *Commentaria in Secundam Secundae Divi Thomae de Aquino* (1518), in II–II, q. 61, a. 1.

10   "Triplex exigitur ordo: ordo partium ad totum, ordo totius ad partes, ordo partis ad partem. Primum respicit justitia legalis quae ordinat subditos ad rempublicam; secundum, justitia distributiva, quae ordinat rempublicam ad subditos; tertium, justitia commutativa quae ordinat privatum ad privatum": B.-H. Merkelbach, *Summa theologiae moralis* (Paris: 1938), vol. II, nos. 252, 253.

that legal justice is primarily a virtue of the government (*princeps*).[11] Presumably,[12] Aquinas' underlying thesis is that this (primarily) governmental responsibility of ordering private things and matters to common good is to be carried out by government and law partly by distributive justice—appropriately converting what is common into what is appropriated and thus "private"—and partly by supervising (by no means necessarily *managing*) dealings between individuals so as to guarantee and mold the requirements of commutative justice with an eye to common good. In any case, little of this concerns what the modern tradition thought of as legal justice: a citizen's allegiance.[13]

A late articulation of this post-Cajetanic tradition is sec. 2411 of the *Catechism of the Catholic Church* ([1992], 1995): "One distinguishes *commutative* justice [which regulates exchanges between persons and between institutions in accordance with a strict respect for their rights] from *legal justice* which concerns what the citizen owes in fairness [*équitablement*: *aequitative*] to the community, and from *distributive* justice which regulates what the community owes its citizens in proportion to their contributions and needs."[14] This is quite distant from St. Thomas.

So del Vecchio proposed, in effect, that it was the eclipse of Aquinas' category or conception of legal—that is general—justice, and its replacement

11 *ST* II–II q. 58 a. 6c: iustitia legalis est specialis virtus secundum suam essentiam, secundum quod respicit commune bonum ut proprium obiectum. Et sic *est in principe principaliter et quasi architectonice*, in subditis autem secundario et quasi ministrative.

12 "Presumably," for it is not certain that Aquinas' treatment of all this is wholly coherent, and, as I argue in *Aquinas*, 187–88, 215–17 (see also del Vecchio, *Justice*, 57 n.2), the focus on forms or kinds (species, etc.) of justice can obscure the issues and the principles of their solution.

13 However, legal/general justice as Aquinas conceives it certainly includes the citizen's receptiveness to and cooperation with any proper legal or governmental arrangements of this kind, and even a willingness of the citizen property-holder to volunteer his *superflua* to the service of the poor and, in dire necessity, to make much of his wealth available to those who would otherwise perish.

14 In the *Catechism*, social justice is dealt with quite separately, in sec. 1928, as concerned with "the conditions that allow associations or individuals to obtain what is their due, according to their nature and their vocation."

(under the same name) with a much thinner category and conception focused on the citizen's duty *as subject*, that stimulated nineteenth-century thinkers, and in due course Pius XI and his advisers, to fill the gap with the new term. Social justice is thus, like Aquinas' legal justice, a responsibility in the first instance of law and government, bearing on private property and transactions,[15] and directed towards securing the common good of the political community. That common good importantly includes the justice of treating like cases alike and different cases differently: the proportionate equality that, by including a proportionate measure of inequality, avoids the inequality (inequity) of treating significantly different cases equally.[16] But the common good also includes, as *Quadragesimo anno* brings out in the passage cited above, the flourishing of particular institutions and arrangements required for a sustainable community and for the flourishing of its members. So social justice's appropriate content is shaped by attention to institutions and arrangements whose appropriateness is not measured simply by considerations of equality but also, and (it seems) primarily, by considerations of worth and need, such as the basic good of marriage as matrix for the procreation and education of children and special friendship and lifelong mutual support of the spouses.

This is at some distance from Millian social justice insofar as the latter is concerned only with equality of "desert."[17] It is far distant from the loose

15 This was underlined by Pius XI in his encyclical *Divini Redemptoris* (1937): [51] ". . . besides commutative justice, there is also social justice with its own set obligations, from which neither employers nor workingmen can escape. Now it is of the very essence of social justice to demand from each individual all that is necessary for the common good." [The English translation on the Vatican website reads "demand *for* each individual," but this is a sheer error, as the Latin, Italian, and other versions make clear: ". . . praeter iustitiam, quam commutativam vocant, socialis etiam iustitia colenda est, quae quidem ipsa officia postulat, quibus neque artifices neque heri se subducere possunt. Atqui socialis iustitiae est id omne *ab singulis exigere*, quod ad commune bonum necessarium sit."]

16 See Plato, *Laws* VI: 757; also V: 744b–c.9

17 Taken to its extreme development, this conception lands us in G. A. Cohen's "luck egalitarianism," the thesis that justice (he might have said "social justice") requires the elimination of all inequalities arising from luck (as distinct from the consequences of choices—from Mill's "desert"). Cohen's master exempli-

modern idea of social justice as something that can be read off from the depiction or structure of a state of affairs, so that the sheer fact of wide disparities of (say) wealth or educational attainment can be declared to be in itself contrary to social justice.[18] Rather, social justice should be understood as the virtue of looking to the common good of all—a virtue in the first instance[19] of rulers (including citizens so far as they participate in rulership as voters)—bearing in mind the conditions of the community's sustainability and flourishing, and accordingly adjusting arrangements, not least private arrangements (say, of property rights, contracts of employment, and so forth), so that they will tend systematically and more adequately to foster and protect decisions and actions promotive of that common good in the circumstances of the community's ongoing existence.

fication is the scenario in which irremovable and non-transferable but destructible manna falls from heaven into Jane's possession, but nobody else's, in a peacefully anarchic state of nature. What justice calls for, says Cohen, is that Jane destroy her manna rather than make use of it (a use that could only be to her benefit alone): G. A. Cohen, *On the Currency of Egalitarian Justice and Other Essays in Political Philosophy* (ed. Michael Otsuka) (Princeton University Press, 2011), 229. Though the analogy between talent and manna is far from perfect, it is close enough to suggest what is involved in luck egalitarianism, in which (in principle) it is better to destroy human good rather than allow it to be participated in unequally.

18 *CCC* 1938 comes questionably and regrettably close to such an approach, very widespread in secular society.

19 This phrase hides some complexities. The duty of individual owners to distribute their *superflua*—a duty of justice insisted upon by St. Thomas (see Finnis, *Aquinas*, 190–96) and the modern Popes under terms such as "the social mortgage on property")—is one which in the first instance is a duty of the owner; but it is one which in most social conditions can only be reasonably and effectively exercised if it is coordinated by government and law (e.g., by way of properly calibrated and administered redistributive taxation).

Chapter Five

The Search for Universal Ethics:
The Church, Natural Law, and Social Justice

Joseph Koterski, S.J.

Fordham University

Among the many ecclesial documents that have some bearing on the question of social justice, two were published in 2009: the papal encyclical letter *Caritas in veritate* and the report from the International Theological Commission entitled "In Search of a Universal Ethic: A New Look at the Natural Law."

The encyclical, the third of Benedict XVI's pontificate, provides an occasion for the pope to extend the lines of thinking about Catholic Social Teaching that he began in *Deus caritas est*. The focus of this document is not restricted to social justice, but he does directly address this topic a number of times in the course of the new encyclical. Although the document from the International Theological Commission does not concentrate on Catholic Social Teaching so much as on natural law, it does make occasional reference to this body of thought, including the topic of social justice. It argues that a proper understanding of the natural moral law and of social justice needs to have its grounding in a rich sense of divine providence as well as in a comprehensive account of human nature and must make good use of the concept of right reasoning.[1] Seen in this way, the natural moral law provides a sound basis for offering a universalistic ethic and a view of social justice to other cultures and religious traditions.

---

1   For a book-length study of the need to have at the basis of any sound theory of the natural moral law this triadic basis of theology, anthropology, and realist epistemology, see Russell Hittinger, *First Grace* (Wilmington, DE: ISI Books, 2002).

The thesis of this paper is that by documents such as these Pope Benedict XVI is not only reaffirming the importance of social justice within the corpus of Catholic Social Teaching but also insisting on the need to correct an unfortunate tendency that isolates within separate silos the three substantive areas of social concern that instead need to be integrated components of authentic Catholic doctrine in this field: the economic, the political, and the cultural (including marriage, family, and society).

1. The Historical Context

Caritas in veritate is the more adventurous document of the two, not only because it must necessarily engage in the difficult task of prudential reasoning that is invariably involved in attempts to apply the principles of Catholic Social Teaching to practical problems, but also by reason of certain novelties—at least in emphasis—in the type of argumentation that it provides. The distinctiveness that I see in this document pertains especially to the type of interpretation that it offers for an earlier papal document (*Populorum progressio*) and thereby its effort to correct a tendency to treat the three areas of social doctrine in separate silos—for instance, when questions of social justice are handled as if unrelated to issues about marriage, family life, and the protection of human life at all the stages of its development. The encyclical is also distinctive (though not unique) in the special stress it lays on certain themes that are often associated with the approach to philosophy generally typical of Thomistic personalism, such as the effort to find in the notion of the dignity of the human person an effective way to make a natural law argument in the present day.

In passing, let me acknowledge that the emergence of the silo problem may be inadvertently related to the way in which the modern corpus of Catholic Social Teaching evolved, and not just the result of recent disputes about political ideology, left and right, however much those disputes may have exacerbated the problem. The encyclicals and other genres of ecclesiastical documents that articulate Catholic Social Teaching are not exempt from the problem that faces every writer: one simply cannot say everything at once, and in some venues one has to make certain assumptions without explicitly discussing them. A writer has to choose to put emphasis on one thing rather than another, and then decide on how to develop the point to sufficient depth. Invariably one will assume various things about the context, on the presumption that one's audience will also take them for granted. But even in the original audience, and all the more so as time goes along, it is not to be expected that everyone will grant those assumptions, or even be aware of them. In time it may become necessary to defend in turn the points that one hoped to presume by giving distinct arguments for their truth. Ideally, in making the later statements, one will be able to point out the latent connections between one set of concerns and the other. I cannot help but think that something like this may have occurred in regard to Catholic Social Teaching over the decades since the beginning of its modern presentation in the encyclicals of Pope Leo XIII.[2]

Over the entire course of its history, from the Apostolic times on, Catholic Social Teaching has recurrently been concerned with all three of its central components (the economic, the political, and the cultural). One may be singled out for special attention in one age or another, depending on time and place. But Leo XIII undertook something truly new in the form that he used for his teaching on these matters, and it is evident not only in the economic concerns of *Rerum novarum* in 1891 but also in his eight prior encyclicals on the political order. The changed world order (e.g., the emergence of secularism as a replacement for the juridical order called Christendom) that he was addressing was the result of various political revolutions, the industrial revolution, the scientific and technological revolutions of the age, the massive social migration from the farms to the cities, and the enormous social dislocations concomitant with these changes. The issues that Leo XIII addressed ranged from the burden of long and tiring workdays for the new factory laborers, through the effects of demon rum, to the systemic threats of atheistic communism and socialism, especially in the politics of labor organizers. Further, he needed to address the rise of secular orders of law and the shift from the *ancien regime* and aristocratic privilege, with their various national churches (e.g., Anglican, Josephinist, Gallican), and the loss of the papal states. Building on *Aeterni patris* (1879)

---

2   For a rich presentation of this tradition, see *Compendium of the Social Doctrine of the Church*, Pontifical Council for Justice and Peace, Libreria Editrice Vaticana (Washington, D.C.: United States Conference of Catholic Bishops, 2004).

and *Gravissimum educationis* (1880), Pope Leo XIII gave articulation to the modern form of Catholic Social Teaching in 1891 when he defended the right to hold private property against communist collectivism, envisioned a Christian form of labor unions to combat the socialist efforts to sweep labor into revolutionary forms of workers' unions, and urged the need for labor and capital to cooperate for the good of both, in a new social order.

The continued practice of concentrating, for instance, just on economic matters in some encyclicals may explain the current but unfortunate manner of presenting Catholic Social Teaching as overwhelmingly economic, and thus something only secondarily political in nature and something that gives only indirect attention to cultural and life issues. The perceived problems of the day were admittedly economic and social, along with the perceived threat to institutional religion. The Enlightenment's attack on the truth-claims of the Catholic religion was also recognized, but it tended to be handled in separate documents, for the pressing problem in the social arena was economic, and that topic got the bulk of the attention in encyclicals like *Rerum Novarum*. In treating economic problems, a certain understanding of the nature of the family could at this point simply be assumed without further comment, given the urgency of dealing with such issues as the propensity to treat workers as raw material, as merely one more commodity whose value was subject entirely to the law of supply and demand. The earlier documents in the modern tradition accordingly exhibit little sense of the need to defend the goodness of the traditional family against alternative lifestyles, or to defend the right to life against attack from those who claim the right to abortion, or to defend embryonic life as a matter of social justice from attacks based on a utilitarian conception of biotechnology. When these issues later arose, they were treated in a separate stream of documents that have little explicit comment on economic or political matters. With Pope Pius XI we get distinct documents for marriage and family issues (e.g., *Casti connubii*, 1930) and for economic matters and social reconstruction (e.g., *Quadragesimo anno*, 1931), as Pius' way of defending the integrity of the family from being broken up under the pressure of work, relocation, long hours, child labor, children without adequate parental supervision and nurture, and so on. The Catholic response to the perceived problems was as comprehensive as possible at each stage of its articulation, but the focus of individual documents tends to be on one problem rather than another. One can also see this trend in other encyclicals of Leo XIII and Pius XI; there are distinct documents that address Christian labor unions, male and female social organizations, the establishment of a system of Catholic parochial schools, etc.

Pope Benedict XVI's encyclical *Caritas in veritate* may well signal a papal decision to make an effort at showing believers the need for religious unity on the various sorts of social issues. This effort is presumably shaped by a sense that the social order will be better protected if there is a more tightly unified front within Catholicism, and as much as possible within all of Christianity, rather than a situation in which hostile forces only need to engage with one portion of the Christian sector and not another, and thus can more easily amass the forces needed to prevail against a house divided.

The document on natural law from the International Theological Commission exhibits some of the same traits as Benedict's encyclical in its effort to engage other traditions and cultures on the question of a universal ethics. The search for a universal ground for morality among diverse cultures is consonant with the basic natural law project. Among the standard claims often made in the classical presentation of the natural moral law are these: (1) although the extent to which the natural moral law is known varies across times and cultures, the natural moral law itself transcends historical periods and cultural origins, and (2) the natural moral law is largely coincident with divine law as disclosed in what is recognized by Christians and Jews to be genuine revelation. Divine law, by this reading, makes explicit by revelation many of the things that any reasonable person and culture ought to be able to discern about morality. Amid the document's highly traditional account of the natural moral law, especially as found in the thought of Thomas Aquinas, the text is noteworthy for its presentation of these standard natural law claims as likely to be advantageous not only for the outreach to other traditions in the quest for a universalist ethics (the specific purpose of the document) but also for showing their relevance to questions of social justice and, more generally, to Catholic Social Teaching.

2. Caritas in veritate

Like Elisha assuming the mantle of Elijah, Pope Benedict XVI clearly undertook to carry on many of the initiatives inaugurated by his predecessor

Pope John Paul II, especially in regard to the proper interpretation of the Second Vatican Council. In opposition both to those who rejected the Council as a revolutionary break from what came before and to those who have even seen it as some kind of license for reinventing the Church, John Paul II repeatedly tried to uphold continuity where others have drawn diametrically opposed conclusions about the Council.[3] Presumably what has elicited this stance has been the fact that the same type of judgment—the claim of radical discontinuity between pre- and post-Vatican II religion—has paradoxically appeared from the pens of figures at both of the extreme ends of the spectrum.

Some of these individuals, for instance, claim that there was a fundamental break in matters of liturgy, and then cheer or jeer according to their tastes. Others propose that there has come to be a radical discontinuity in regard to ecclesial authority. They either treat the Church as a pervasively democratic institution or they bemoan wimpish failures to ensure adequate ecclesial discipline. Yet others—and these are particularly relevant for our present purposes—have argued that the Church has moved away from the allegedly outmoded categories of natural law thinking typical of the preconciliar period. Some await the day when there will be full acceptance of the moral implications of recognizing individual experience as legitimately decisive for the choices one faces, especially in difficult cases. Some look to the more undisciplined forms of personalism for grounds supporting the acceptance of practices that have been traditionally considered immoral and even their recognition as fundamental rights; others see in personalist thinking only a failure in moral nerve to address what they think already perfectly clear from considerations of natural law and thus in no need of revision. It is thus no surprise that some also see a comparable gulf between pre- and post-conciliar periods in regard to Catholic Social Teaching. In that light some evaluate the ongoing developments in this tradition by John Paul II and now Benedict XVI as pure naiveté, if not some plot to provide the bulwark of ecclesial authority for a liberal agenda in the socio-political order. Others take the occasional references to natural law in these documents as mere window dressing and papal sentimentality, while the really

---

3 See his pre-papal book *Sources of Renewal* as well as his many comments on this subject during the period of his papacy.

crucial material is to be found in the practical judgments and proposals for action that occur elsewhere. It is this tendency to think in terms of silos that texts like the encyclical *Caritas in veritate* seem intended to challenge.

As the ancient saying has it, *in medio virtus stat*. Our recent popes have repeatedly urged us to see the continuity of the Church's doctrine before, during, and after the Second Vatican Council. Doing so allows us to understand the Catholic religion, in all of its truth and beauty, to be what will reform Catholic culture in the most authentic sense of reform.[4]

It is significant, I think, that Benedict XVI commences his third encyclical with an explicit corrective to the notion that the ongoing development of post-conciliar Catholic Social Teaching in recent decades differs radically from the Church's pre-conciliar doctrine (see CV sec. 12). Bearing in mind the historical occasion for this encyclical allows us to understand the context for these comments. It was issued to commemorate the fortieth anniversary of the 1967 *Populorum progressio* (admittedly, the document only manages to observe the anniversary belatedly, for the encyclical was issued in 2009). It was the twentieth anniversary of that document in 1987 that John Paul II used for the delivery of one of his social encyclicals, *Sollicitudo rei socialis*. As evident in Pius XI's way of using the fortieth anniversary of the 1891 *Rerum novarum* for his 1931 *Quadragesimo anno*, the papal remembrance of documentary anniversaries is not simply celebratory or sentimental; rather, the intent sometimes proves to be respectfully corrective in nature. Pius XI, for instance, quietly replaces with more authentically Thomistic notions some elements that Leo XIII used to articulate the concept of property in *Rerum novarum* that risk being too much connected to the social contract thought of John Locke. He also pushes the Leonine idea of a "living wage" (articulated mostly in terms of what an individual worker needs) toward the more challenging notion of a "family wage," and he

---

4   There have been a number of books that address this issue from a modernist viewpoint, including the five-volume series entitled *History of Vatican II* edited by Giuseppe Alberigo and Joseph A. Komonchak et al. (Orbis, 1996–), and John W. O'Malley's *What Happened at Vatican II?* (The Belknap Press of Harvard University Press, 2008). Among those who stress the continuity is Agostino Marchetto's *The Second Vatican Ecumenical Council: A Counterpoint for the History of the Council*, translated by Kenneth D. Whitehead (Scranton, PA: University of Scranton Press, 2010).

develops the new principle of subsidiarity from various hints on that subject within Thomism.

Benedict XVI not only continues but advances the project of John Paul II by showing the profound continuity of the Church's Social Teaching before and after the Council. In general, where John Paul II tends to make *Gaudium et spes* and *Dignitatis humanae* his fundamental reference points, Benedict has preferred to concentrate on *Dei verbum* and *Sacrosanctum concilium*. And yet he shows a willingness to engage the question of social justice that is central both to the conciliar document *Gaudium et spes* and to the social encyclical that so closely followed the Council, *Populorum progressio*. That document is widely thought to adopt much of the optimism typical of *Gaudium et spes* about the prospect for genuine social progress by the application of new financial resources, human intelligence, and creativity to social problems as then perceived. In addition to criticizing excessively narrow visions of human development in *Sollicitudo rei socialis*, John Paul II used the occasion to develop the idea of solidarity.

In his turn, Benedict XVI is once again using the opportunity of commemorating *Populorum progressio* to offer some further correctives, specifically by trying to develop in new ways the personalist idea of generosity as a possible root for thinking, among other things, about social justice and in general the social order. Despite the suspicions raised about personalism in some quarters, papal documents thus continue to embrace and develop the notion in interesting ways.

It is by no means unexpected that the demands of papal courtesy would preclude any direct criticism of a predecessor's ideas. But it is also quite typical of papal thinking to stress the need for the proper interpretation of statements made in earlier papacies. This courteous form of papal respect for previous papal documents is evident in this encyclical through the stress laid on distinguishing the non-negotiable principles present in that document from what is presumably better taken as prudential reasoning. Even though there are also prudential judgments that are made in *Caritas in veritate* (and some of them of a relatively adventurous sort), the relatively lower levels of expectation about whether they will be accepted (in comparison to the high level of respect expected for perennially valid principles) needs to be carefully noted. I take the effort to ascertain the level of authority operative for various statements within a given document to be much akin to the work that regularly needs to be undertaken generally and across the board in theological reflection on magisterial statements from councils as well as popes when trying to determine the degree of assent that is due any one of them. In times past the results of this discernment have led to use of a range of categories from what must be regarded as "infallible teaching" to what is "not offensive to pious ears."

Some of the statements found near the beginning of *Populorum progressio* (see esp. sec.14–21) stress that the Christian vision of development should not be limited to merely economic growth and must promote the good of every human being and of the whole person in order to be thought authentic. But almost all the rest of that document and of its companion piece *Octagesima adveniens* of 1971 concern the technical analysis of the economic sphere and considered practical proposals in this area. Noting the difference between these two types of statement enables one to sort out the non-negotiable principles that the document is acknowledging from its important but nonetheless prudential judgments. Like part four of John Paul II's *Sollicitudo rei socialis*, chapter one of *Caritas in veritate* stresses that authentic human development includes but is much larger than the economic sphere. In lines reminiscent of *Deus caritas est* (see esp. sec. 27 and 31), *Caritas in veritate* (see sec. 14) mounts a critique of utopian ideologies that threaten economic development as well as human life in general. Benedict even finds ways to praise *Octagesima adveniens* (OA) and *Evangelii nuntiandi* (EN) for similar positions (see CV sec. 14–15 commenting on OA sec. 30–42 and EN §31), and especially *Populorum progressio* (sec. 42) for sounding the theme that development must "promote the good of every man and of the whole man" in order to be genuine (CV sec. 18).

But throughout the development of this and related points about social justice in chapters two through six, Benedict's encyclical employs two correlative strategies that are both of a corrective nature. One is the restraint it clearly wants to impose upon the quasi-Pelagian tendencies that an Augustinian like Benedict apparently detects in optimism about the prospects for the achievement of social justice by government intervention into the economy in the name of social justice of the sort that was often championed in the era of *Gaudium et spes* and *Populorum progressio*. The other is the need for special care in protecting the cultural dimensions of the social order (including the defense of human life) in the course of his work to make a sound distinction between the demands of social justice and those of social charity. It is no surprise that this deeply Augustinian thinker stresses the difference between social justice and social charity in the very act of formulating the source of the distinct types of obligation that we have regarding the social order.

Whether we consider the differences between Paul VI's expectations and those that Benedict enunciates in chapter two of *Caritas in veritate*, or look to Benedict's characteristic stress on the lack of a living sense of God in much of contemporary culture (an important focus for the analysis of poverty that he provides at length in chapter five of this encyclical, e.g., sec. 56), we find at no point a merely abstract sense of social justice. This is to say that he regards questions of social justice as important, but not the sole or even the chief determinant of the proper practical application of Catholic Social Teaching. For Benedict, we also need to bring in the distinct demands of social charity. There are plenty of examples given of social justice questions: for instance, the discussions of the right of access to food and water in sec. 27, of free markets and their inevitably commercial logic in sec. 35 and sec. 71, of the environment and ecology in sec. 48–49, and of technology in sec. 59–60 and sec. 70–71. But Benedict's encyclical never allows any of these issues to be treated in isolation from the life-issues and from the sphere of culture that has always been the third great focus of Catholic Social Teaching along with the sphere of economics and politics. Further, he recurrently reminds us that respect for the obligations of social charity will need to be weighed, especially in view of the inevitable limitations of ensuring justice by even the best forms of civil authority.

For instance, in the same paragraph where the encyclical comments on the need for a network of institutions that can guarantee regular access to food and water as well as the capital that is needed to promote sustainable development (sec. 27), he gives unmistakable importance to the life-issues: "The right to food, like the right to water, has an important place within the pursuit of other rights, beginning with the fundamental right to life." Respect for life can never be detached from questions concerning social justice and the development of peoples, and he argues that programs for material and economic development—long thought to be the engines for the achievement of social justice—should never promote contraception or abortion, sterilization or euthanasia.

Similarly, Benedict works against any silo-approach to the discussion of environmental concerns and ecology in chapter four. In the same chapter he treats extensively the question of the "inalienable values" of life, traditional marriage, and family in the course of arguing that population increases should not be seen as the primary cause of underdevelopment and that a responsible openness to life is a rich social and economic resource. The argument that he makes here shows his sense of the deep interconnection of these issues, as when he notes that nations whose birthrates have declined below replacement level are generally experiencing the expected consequences of contraception, e.g., added strain on welfare systems, lack of workers, and especially the impoverished relations of disordered family life.

His sustained repudiation of the silo-tendency is again evident in the paragraph that ends chapter four:

> If there is a lack of respect for the right to life and to a natural death, if human conception, gestation, and birth are made artificial, if human embryos are sacrificed to research, the conscience of society ends up losing the concept of human ecology and, along with it, that of environmental ecology. It is contradictory to insist that future generations respect the natural environment when our educational systems and laws do not help them to respect themselves. (sec. 51)

One could also adduce here the stance that this encyclical presents in its repudiation of *in vitro* fertilization, research that is destructive of embryos, cloning, and the manufacture of hybrids. Citing Paul VI, Benedict argues that the question of social justice is at root an anthropological question that intrinsically concerns how life is created and manipulated, and never just a question of economic development (sec. 74–76).

The paragraphs of *Caritas in veritate* that concentrate most fully on the application of the principles of distributive justice and solidarity to the free market system (e.g., §35) correct not only the notion that economics could ever possibly be rightly regarded as autonomous and independent of moral evaluation, but also the correlative notion that was so popular in the wake of *Gaudium et spes* and *Populorum progressio* that the state with its "logic of public obligation" could alone suffice to correct the excesses of the "logic of exchange" so prominent in the market economy. There must also be a "logic of civil society" that involves generosity, concern for the common good, and social charity (see, e.g., CV sec. 39 and DCE sec. 30–31).

Much like his predecessor John Paul II, Benedict XVI is deeply appreciative of the possibilities of responsible self-government, but perhaps (especially in his allusions to Alexis de Tocqueville's *Democracy in America*) he is even more deeply alert than his predecessor to the possibilities of the tyranny of the majority. He had sounded this warning note in sec. 28–29 of *Deus caritas est*, and does so now again in sec. 55–57 of *Caritas in veritate*. In the former document he argues at length that the state (whatever the type of regime) is responsible for developing and maintaining some adequate system of justice, even if no civil state should ever be expected to be able to secure perfect justice or to eliminate the ongoing need for social charity by individuals and by the Church. His argument there is as follows.

There are two fundamental principles that need to be remembered in this regard: (1) the just ordering of society and the state is a central responsibility of politics, but (2) charity will always be needed. On the first point, he affirms that justice is both the aim and the intrinsic criterion of political life. There is a proper autonomy to the temporal sphere, and the state must guarantee religious freedom and must respect the independence of the Church, the social embodiment of Christian faith. Catholic Social Teaching provides a way for faith to instruct and clarify human reasoning, but makes no claim that the Church should have power over the state. By arguing on the basis of reason and natural law, Catholic Social Teaching can help to form consciences and encourage justice.

Respect for the second principle provides the needed balance here. Love (*caritas*) will always be indispensable, even in relatively well-ordered societies, for there will always be aspects of the situation that elude the administration of justice. Recognizing the obligations of charity will enable us to address suffering and other concerns. While the formation of just structures in law, government, and economics is *not directly* the duty of the Church but the sphere of statesmen and the work of politics, the Church— the pope points out—does have an *indirect* duty to assist in purifying human reasoning and in reawakening the moral forces without which just structures will never be established or maintained. The Christian lay faithful have a *direct* duty to work for a just ordering of society, for they have obligations in justice as citizens of the state and they must work for the common good, according to their ability and their state in life. The Church's charitable organizations are an indispensable aspect of her own nature and life, and they assist the faithful in developing a life of service in charity to those in need.

In *Caritas in veritate* we find not only this important distinction between the state's duties to promote justice and the Church's need to promote charity (see sec. 53–67) but also what may be an effort by Benedict to suggest the possibility of a new kind of natural law argument. If this is the correct reading of the document, the proposal is one that is deeply consistent with the traditional theory of the natural moral law but perhaps without some of the "heavy baggage" that the term "natural law" carries in some quarters. There was a comparable effort, I think, on the part of John Paul II to undertake a similar initiative that is profoundly consonant with traditional natural law reasoning by his development of the theology of the body and his theory of the spousal meaning of sexual communion. To suggest, as the theology of the body does, that there is an intrinsic meaning to our bodies, to our bodily actions, and especially to sexual relations and to the nature of marriage, is to propose a way to see moral obligation as arising from human nature and to see the directedness of human embodiment and human sociality as providing grounds for ethical normativity. This is, at its heart, a strategy of argument that is deeply at one with the reasoning typical of traditional natural law theory precisely by virtue of the fact that it finds in the teleology or inner directedness of nature the normative grounds for obligation, virtue, and proper life-orientation, but I will not attempt to defend that view any further here.

In the present document we find the use of terminology and of a structure of argumentation that seems, in one respect, deeply personalist in character. As with the personalist focus of the moral writings of John Paul II, this human dignity-based approach can serve to gain the considerable rhetorical advantages of modern personalism for what remains fundamentally a natural law argument. Ever since Kant, personalist arguments have exhibited an immediate appeal to many people: namely, one may never treat a person as a mere means but must always respect persons as ends in themselves.[5] And yet much of the heavy lifting in such arguments still needs to done by recourse to human nature, as is the case in traditional natural law ethics. This situation is true not only of the recent tradition of papal personalism but also in a number of twentieth-century Thomistic personalists, including figures like Jacques Maritain and W. Norris Clarke, S.J., not to mention the pre-papal Karol Wojtyła.

The appeal to the dignity of the person can with relative ease garner assent for the notion that there are certain basic and inviolable human rights that must be respected for any and all persons. At first this assent seems to require no additional argumentation beyond the apparently self-evident statement that anything that is personal should be respected as having the rights of a person. But upon further consideration, it seems to me that its intuitive grounding of rights in persons puts the focus on individuals whose personhood is obvious and undeniable and that this could inadvertently limit its coverage to those beings already somehow recognized as obviously persons. Its coverage does not necessarily extend to the cases nearer the borders. However useful an approach that urges us to see the personal rights of those readily recognized as genuine persons, it does not help us to decide questions of personhood in those cases where there is public dispute about personhood (e.g., the unborn, the disfigured, the profoundly handicapped, the demented). For the resolution of questions about inclusion or exclusion of such individuals within the set of "persons," the discussion needs to return to whether the entities are persons, that is, beings with a personal nature.

In this respect, the discussion turns on a dispute about whether all human beings are persons rather than a question about the rights of any being that is a person. The resolution of this question in favor of the personhood of the unborn and the senile and other human beings whom some do not intuitively recognize as persons (especially when personhood is implicitly or explicitly conceived of in terms of presently functional capabilities rather than in terms of the nature that supports such capabilities) is questionable today. Seen in this way, personalist arguments for respecting human rights and human dignity only work comprehensively for all human

---

5   Consider, for instance, *Totality and Infinity* and other works of Emmanuel Levinas.

persons when there is also in play a highly metaphysical insight about the difference between (1) all persons (including all those beings that are by their nature persons even if only nascent in the unfolding of their specifically personal powers and abilities and not just those that are intuitively obvious as persons because of the actual exercise of their personal capacities when these capacities are sufficiently developed for such personal activities as thinking and freely choosing), and (2) things of any other sort (i.e., nonpersonal beings). It is the nature of embodied persons at any stage of their development or degeneration that is clearly intended here in this document, not the realm of self-constituting persons that is typical of Kantian theories of moral autonomy and that in some authors is apparently restricted to those beings that manifest recognizably personal activities.

Here in Benedict's third encyclical one may also be getting some hints of what may be an argument-pattern that will be further developed in subsequent documents. Early in the third chapter of *Caritas in veritate*, for instance, sec. 34 notes how unappreciated the role of "gift" is in human life and how underutilized the "principle of generosity" is in discussions of morality. To be briefly speculative here, perhaps we would not be too far off to suggest that the incipient idea here is that it is intrinsic to human nature that we are gift-receivers who must also learn to be gift-givers, and that a crucial part of a developing papal vision of "personalist natural law" will include a rich vision of human nature in terms of the needs to give, to receive, and to elicit what is needed from the other. The chapter of the encyclical that follows speculates about the possible application of these insights about the role of generosity in human nature for an understanding of the limited but genuine kind of restraint and guidance that moral principles need to provide to economics and questions about the free market. In sec. 53 there is the same sort of personalist language about the importance of understanding personal growth and the intrinsically social character of human living in terms of "relation," for instance, in the mention of our relationships with other people and with God as crucial for the maturation of personal identity.

Admittedly, the encyclical's argumentation in this direction is still underdeveloped, but its very presence here at all strikes me as typical of the way in which new argumentation has tended to emerge in the course of the tradition of Catholic Social Teaching for other novel concepts, for instance, the idea of the family wage by Pope Pius XI and the concept of solidarity by Pope John Paul II. Even in its incipient forms here, the notions of generosity and relationality as intrinsically important parts of human personal nature suggest quite a new approach but one likely to be quite fruitful because of the significantly different take they make possible on the question of social justice as part of a larger category of social charity, for the encyclical does not rest all of its suggestions about the social order on the notion of justice but frequently turns to the obligations in charity that exceed those of justice. Presumably the argument here is that the demands of justice in the strict sense must not be exaggerated or else the very idea will be brought into contempt as mere code-talk for a welfare state, a form of socialism, envy of the rich, or a call for the redistribution of wealth on the basis of some perceived inequality of possession.

In short, I find myself wondering if one of the aims of this encyclical might be to speculate on the possible utility of this strategy of argument as a new way to articulate some of the social demands of natural law theory, on the basis of an idea of human personal nature, more adequately considered. These last comments are admittedly speculative and need further consideration—perhaps they will be clarified by further installments in the papal tradition.

3. In Search of a Universal Ethic: A New Look at the Natural Law

Let us turn now to an ecclesial text on natural law theory from the same year—a text that does not bear Benedict's authorship but rather comes from the International Theological Commission. To judge from the considerable number of allusions to the natural moral law in Benedict's writings[6]—a number that might seem out of proportion to someone whose thought operated only in the venues of Augustinian and Bonaventurian theology—it would not be surprising to learn that the ITC document is an effort to be responsive to a Benedictine request for renewed consideration of this subject.

---

6   See, for instance, Benedict XVI's address of February 12, 2007, to the International Congress on Natural Moral Law, organized by the Pontifical Lateran University, AAS 99 (2007), p. 244.

For consideration of the topic of social justice, the most significant section of the new document on natural law from the ITC is the fourth chapter ("Natural Law and the *Polis*"), which comments in passing on the question of social justice in the course of its treatment of the social nature of the person. After briefly reviewing the document as a whole, we will take up the thought of this fourth chapter and note in particular the interesting recurrence of the Augustinian distinction between the earthly and heavenly cities as the context for this document's considerations about the need for social charity as well as social justice. Admittedly, the topic of social justice is not the main thrust of the document, and so I offer comments on this document primarily as a supplement to comments on the encyclical. We need to be mindful that this document is significant, but it is not at the same level of authority as the papal encyclical.

The three chapters that precede the discussion of natural law and the *polis* concern, respectively, (1) convergences in matters of morality among the cultures and religions of the world, (2) the universality of the natural moral law, regardless of the terminology used to designate moral insights based on common human nature, and (3) the theoretical foundations of natural law. Following the chapter that needs to be at the center of our focus, there is a short chapter on Jesus Christ as the fulfillment of the natural law. In that chapter I find not only a nod toward the Augustinian and Bonaventurian tendencies to see Christ at the summit of any use of the natural intellect but also, indirectly, a use of a theological approach that is rather typical of *la nouvelle théologie* and the theology of the *Communio* movement, namely, the view that the ultimate ground for claims about the dignity of the human person resides not so much in anything known philosophically such as our nature as human beings, but in something known by revelation, namely, that we are made in the image and likeness of God. There may also be a nod here in the direction of such papal pronouncements as *Dominus Jesus*, a document important as a corrective for certain exaggerated forms of ecumenism. This is clearly a topic of considerable concern to the ITC in its other work and it is especially relevant here, given the extended consideration of convergences among the world's various religions and wisdom-traditions at the start of this document.

Although not from Benedict's hand, the document is quite strikingly Benedictine from the very start. The opening paragraph of the introduction,

for instance, invokes the frequent concern today with planetary environ-
mentalism and human ecology in an effort to ask whether there are objective
moral values capable of uniting human cooperation and procuring "peace
and brotherhood." But the document undertakes discussion of these matters
in the typically Benedictine sense of such phrases as "planetary environmen-
talism" and "human ecology," namely, in a way that resists any possibility of
keeping globalism, ecology, economics, and the life issues in distinct silos.[7]
Even its sympathetic treatment (at ITC sec. 5) of the UN's *Universal Declaration of Human Rights* bemoans the misinterpretation of the idea of human
rights in that document if they are in any way to be separated "from the ethical and rational dimension that constitutes their foundation and end in favor
of a pure utilitarian legalism." In the following paragraphs (ITC sec. 6–7)
the document argues that a minimalist world consensus about the existence
of such rights is insufficient to protect them from relativizing tendencies
and the threat of a tyranny of the majority (the same basic argument from
de Tocqueville that Benedict XVI used in *Deus caritas est* and *Caritas in veritate*):

> Under the pretext that every claim of an objective and universal
> truth could be the source of intolerance and violence and that
> only relativism could safeguard the pluralism of values and
> democracy, a case is made for a juridical positivism that refuses
> references to any objective ontological criterion for what is just.
> In this perspective, the ultimate horizon of right and the moral
> norm is the law in force, which is supposed to be just by defi-
> nition, since it is the will of the legislator. But this opens the
> path to the will of power, to the dictatorship of the numerical
> majority, and to ideological manipulation, to the detriment of
> the common good. (ITC sec. 7)

---

7   For a treatment of Benedict's distinctive handling of ecology and environ-
    mentalism as a kind of natural law argumentation designed to defend the in-
    trinsic dignity of human life, see my "Going in Their Door" in *Fellowship of
    Catholic Scholars Quarterly* 32/3 (2009): 2–3.

The protection of human rights and allied notions of social justice, the document urges (see esp. ITC sec. 9), may find better warrant by "a renewed presentation of the doctrine of natural law." True to its title, the document sees consideration of natural law as suitable for the development of a universalistic ethic: "Christianity does not have the monopoly on the natural law. In fact, founded on the reason common to all, the natural law is the basis of collaboration among all people of good will, whatever their religious convictions" (*ibid.*). But the variety of misunderstandings to which the term "natural law" is subject warrants a careful review of that notion. The document then conducts such a review through noting the "convergences" among the great traditions of philosophical wisdom and the great world religions.

The chapter given to the rehearsal of the cultural and anthropological evidence for common moral values and of the various ways in which people can come to discover the precepts of the natural law as universal and intelligible to anyone of good will follows the lines of argument typical of traditional natural law theory, with abundant citations of Aquinas and the UN Declaration (chapter two). The third chapter, on theoretical foundations, shows a deep appreciation for a rich anthropology and for theological as well as teleological considerations in making the case for the reality of the natural moral law, e.g., in saying:

> The idea of natural law is justified first of all on the level of thoughtful reflection on anthropological constants that characterize a successful humanization of the person and a harmonious social life. . . . Certain forms of behavior are recognized as expressing an exemplary excellence in the way of living and realizing one's humanity. . . . However, only the recognition of the metaphysical dimension of the real can give the natural law its full and complete philosophical justification. In fact, metaphysics allows for the comprehension that the universe does not have in itself its ultimate reason for being, and it manifests the fundamental structure of the real: the distinction between God, the self-subsistent Being and the other beings set forth by Him into existence. . . . The Creator is not only the principle of

creatures but also the transcendent end towards which they tend by nature. (ITC sec. 61–63)

This way of putting the matter is typical of the document's approach, and the interweaving of theological, teleological, and social aspects of the situation makes clear that the document is thoroughly in harmony with the approach championed in *Veritatis splendor*, namely, a view of natural law theory that insists that there be reference to the providence of God as well as to human nature teleologically considered for there to be an adequate and valid notion of the natural moral law.[8]

It is in the fourth chapter that we find the most extensive discussion of the intrinsically social character of human existence (e.g., ITC sec. 84, 86). The document roots social morality in the common good of human persons (ITC sec. 85, 87),[9] as when the document notes:

> By the fact that men have a vocation to live in society with others, they possess in common an assembly of goods to pursue and values to defend. This is what one calls the common good. If the person is an end in himself, the society has the end of promoting, consolidating, and developing its common good. (ITC sec. 85)

In the ensuing paragraphs (ITC sec. 88–90) the document makes clear that it is the set of duties that we have to the common good as a society of persons, each one with the same inalienable dignity, that is the proper source for any assertions about social justice, and not any claims of an egalitarian nature or some abstract set of individual rights, as might be typical of some contemporary political philosophy. In commenting on the way in which these ideas are to be realized in society, one repeatedly sees this basic principle that is at work—for example, in this passage:

8   On this point, see Hittinger, esp. ch. 2.
9   One of the better books that I have discovered on the implications of this point is *Human Goods, Economic Evils: A Moral Approach to the Dismal Science* by Edward Hadas (Wilmington, DE: ISI, 2007).

The natural order of society at the service of the person is indicated . . . by four values that follow from natural inclinations of man and that delineate the contours of the common good that society must pursue, namely, freedom, truth, justice, and solidarity. . . . If one of these becomes absent, the polis tends toward anarchy or the rule of the stronger. . . . Without justice there is no society but only the rule of violence. Justice is the highest good the polis can procure. . . . Society must be governed in a manner of solidarity, securing mutual assistance and responsibility for the destiny of others, and making sure that the goods placed at the society's disposal are able to respond to the needs of all. (ITC sec. 87)

In its comments on how the natural law ought to actualize considerations of social justice, the examples given reach across the spectrum, so as to avoid the silo problem that we discussed above, as in this paragraph:

Positive law must strive to put the requirements of the natural law into action. It does this either by way of conclusion (the natural law forbids murder, the positive law should prohibit abortion), or by way of determination (the natural law prescribes the punishment of the guilty, the positive penal law determinates the punishments to apply for each category of crimes). . . . (ITC sec. 91)

When the document turns back to larger questions of political philosophy, it interestingly takes up the Benedictine use of the Augustinian doctrine of the two cities, especially in explicitly insisting (ITC sec. 96) that the political order must not be confused with the order of grace to which human beings are called to give their free adherence. The political order, rather, is linked to "the universal human ethic inscribed in nature." The goal of the political order must be, so far as possible, to promote justice by procuring "for the persons who comprise it what is necessary for the full realization of their human life, which includes certain values, spiritual and religious, as well as the freedom of citizens to determine themselves with respect to the absolute and supreme goods" (ITC sec. 96).

This Augustinian distinction between the two cities, so typical of Benedict's social encyclicals, is the context for the insistence in the fifth chapter ("Jesus as the Fulfillment of the Natural Law") on the obligations in charity to "a love that is the gift of self" that goes "beyond the rule of justice" (ITC sec. 108). The distinction between the obligations of justice and the obligations of charity is not a denial of the demands of social justice but a reflection on what can and what cannot be legitimately required of all human cultures for the sake of "living together in justice and peace" according to the demands of the natural law (ITC sec. 113). In addition, the knowledge of Christ imposes yet further obligations (not just suggestions or ideals) upon believers in Christ as a matter of social charity, as suggested by reflection on the parable of the Good Samaritan and the Sermon on the Mount (ITC sec. 108).

4. Conclusions

The review of the two documents under study in this paper seems to me to indicate that the Benedictine contribution to Catholic Social Teaching thus far can be summed up under the following theses:

(1) The duties that human beings have as part of social justice are real and urgent, but need to be understood to flow from a sense of the common good and not, say, as part of an agenda determined by current political sensibilities that are derived from a redistributist ideology grounded in philosophical egalitarianism.

(2) Social justice concerns are one part of the justice that the state must seek to realize by adequate systems for the administration of justice. Benedict himself and the recent document issued by the International Theological Commission during his papacy continue to affirm what earlier documents of Catholic Social Teaching tended to call "the universal destination" of the goods of this earth. The documents under study here tend to discuss this point under the terminology of the common good.

(3) Benedict's devotion to the basically Augustinian understanding of the two cities supports the distinction that he invokes between the obligations of social justice and social charity as distinct sources of moral obligation.

Chapter Six
Social Justice, Charity,
and Catholic Social Doctrine
Robert G. Kennedy
University of St. Thomas

According to the Second Vatican Council, the particular vocation of the lay faithful is to penetrate and perfect the temporal order with the spirit of the Gospel.[1] Though it aims at the same objective, the salvation of all men and women, this vocation is quite different in its means from, though complementary to, the vocation of the ordained clergy (who focus on the instruction, governance, and sanctification of the ecclesial community).[2] In pursuing this vocation, the laity ought to be formed in their thinking, and perhaps even directed in their action, by the teaching of the Church. More specifically, they ought to learn and take to heart the social doctrine of the Church and apply it carefully to the circumstances in which they live and work.[3] This is sound counsel but much more difficult to act upon than one might suppose. In many fields of human knowledge fundamental concepts and terms are precisely defined and commonly accepted. The natural

---

1   Second Vatican Council, "Decree on the Apostolate of the Laity" (*Apostolicam actuositatem*), 1965, no. 2.

2   See, for example, the distinctions drawn in the apostolic exhortation of Pope John Paul II, "On the Vocation and Mission of the Lay Faithful" (*Christifideles laici*), 1988, no. 21–23. The principal vocation of ordained ministers is internally focused, to serve the people of God, while the vocation of the laity is externally focused.

3   See Pope John XXIII, "Christianity and Social Progress" (*Mater et magistra*), 1961, no. 236.

sciences are a model for this but similar clarity is found in many other fields, such as law, architecture, engineering, business (particularly in finance and accounting) and medicine. Professionals in these fields—and this is one of the marks of the professional—understand and accept the definition of basic concepts. This is not to say that there is no disagreement at all but rather that the basic concepts are well known and generally accepted.[4] The social doctrine of the Church, however, is different. Unlike these professional fields, and even unlike some other areas of theology, the fundamental concepts and terms are generally not precisely defined nor are they commonly accepted. As a result, there is a considerable degree of ambiguity in the field that complicates practical efforts to shape the temporal order. This is further complicated by the fact that most official documents in this area have a pastoral character, which lends itself to a rather casual use of terms.

Furthermore, the Church's social doctrine itself lacks an essential unity. This is not to say that its elements are in irresolvable conflict with one another but rather that the formal teaching of the Church has been expressed in discrete bits and pieces, written at different times for different purposes. No official effort has been made to draw these elements together into a coherent and unified whole, nor is there even common agreement about which official statements are authentic components of the Church's social teaching.[5]

With that in mind, the objective of this paper is to consider the foundations of the Church's teaching on the good society, how an evolving

4   Some considerable amount of professional energy is devoted in many fields to refining and updating commonly accepted definitions and principles. Consider, for example, the controversy surrounding the recent publication of the *Diagnostic and Statistical Manual of Mental Disorders* (DMS 5).

5   The *Compendium of the Social Doctrine of the Church*, which was published by the Vatican in 2004, represents the only serious effort to date by the Church to assemble and articulate its social teaching in a unified fashion. On one level, it is a very fine document and it will be widely consulted for many years. On another level, though, it is quite selective about the topics it treats and the sources it considers. For example, the problem of the proper relationship between civil and ecclesiastical authorities, which occupied the Church at the highest levels for centuries, is hardly treated. Nor is there an agreed-upon list of documents that can be considered "social," even among the encyclicals of the past century or so.

notion of social justice has moved beyond those foundations, and how a renewed appreciation of the importance of charity can restore practical integrity to the Church's teaching.

1. Catholic Social Thought: Tradition or Doctrine?

Given that ambiguities abound in the social tradition, perhaps a place to
begin to resolve some of these ambiguities is to clarify what does and does
not belong to the teaching of the Church. In this regard, we use a number
of terms loosely and interchangeably. We speak about the Catholic social
tradition, Catholic social *thought*, Catholic social *teaching*, and Catholic social
doctrine as if each of these terms refers to the same body of, what shall we
say, knowledge? thinking?

Let me propose a more precise distinction, which I think actually reflects the current practice of the Church. I will use the phrase "Catholic
social *doctrine*" to refer to a body of teaching on social questions either articulated or deliberately appropriated by the Magisterium and proposed to
Catholics for their acceptance in faith.[6] (I will take Catholic social doctrine
and Catholic social teaching to be synonymous.) Some of its elements are
ancient—Augustine and Aquinas have been hugely influential—but the
dramatic political and economic changes beginning in the late eighteenth
century provoked a body of reflections and responses from Pope Gregory
XVI (1831–1846) to Pope Leo XIII (1878–1903) and each of their succes-
sors. These documents, along with statements from synods of bishops and
other sources (e.g., dicasteries of the Holy See), constitute the modern expression of the Church's social doctrine. While much attention has been
given in the twentieth century to economic issues, the subjects addressed
in these documents range much more widely. Indeed, most of the documents of the nineteenth century concern political issues, particularly the
relationship and limits of civil and ecclesiastical authority.

---

6   It is worth noting that no element of the social doctrine of the Church has
     ever been formally defined by pope or council. Nevertheless, this doctrine
     ought to be accepted by faithful Catholics with the "religious assent" and "sub-
     mission of mind and will" that is called for by the Second Vatican Council,
     Dogmatic Constitution on the Church (*Lumen gentium*) no. 25.

Furthermore, we also need to recognize that this social doctrine is rooted in and draws upon the discipline of Catholic moral theology. The principles of the social doctrine, therefore, must be consistent with the settled moral doctrine of the Church, and this latter discipline must be one of the keys for interpreting concepts and statements in documents on social doctrine.[7]

Over against this official social doctrine we can identify what we might call the Catholic social *tradition* (which I will take to be synonymous with Catholic social *thought*). This tradition comprises elements concerning the political, economic, and cultural dimensions of social life. It is a theological discipline of sorts, but unlike other theological disciplines (e.g., Christology or sacramental theology), its witnesses include members from throughout the Church, from bishops and priests to consecrated religious to laity in all walks of life. Inevitably, given the complexity of social life and the wide array of these witnesses across temporal, political, and vocational boundaries, the social tradition has failed to develop the coherence that marks other areas of theology. Some of the *social* tradition's elements, or at least some of the views proposed by Catholics who identify with the tradition, may at times be in tension with established elements of the Catholic *moral* tradition.[8]

7   Because of its subject matter, and to some degree because of its methodology, theology has always struggled with a lack of precision in defining concepts and principles. Catholic social *doctrine*, to say nothing of the *tradition*, can be especially loose in its use of terms. Over the last century or more, the popes have often introduced terms in novel context without defining carefully what they meant by these terms. Most recently, for example, Pope Benedict XVI made extensive use of the terms "gratuity" and "gratuitousness" in his ency-clical *Caritas in veritate* (2009) but never offered a definition. A contrast, and three rare exceptions, are Pius XI's definition of "subsidiarity" in *Quadragesimo anno*, no. 79 (1931), John XXIII's definition of the common good in *Mater et magistra*, no. 65, and John Paul II's introduction of the term "solidarity" in *Sollicitudo rei socialis*, no. 38 (1987).

8   Perhaps with these tensions in mind, the Second Vatican Council, in *Gaudium et spes* (no. 43), warned Catholics against claiming that their personal views on social issues carried the authority of the Church. (See also *Mater et magistra*, no. 238.) No one but the pope and the bishops united with him have such au-thority. This points us in the direction of the distinction we ought to be careful to make between the large and somewhat messy Catholic social *tradition,* which often focuses on questions of prudential judgment, and the more limited offi-cial teaching of the Church, which is its social *doctrine*. When, in 2004, the

This happens because the *social* tradition, which ranges more widely and includes so many more voices, is naturally deeply influenced by secular movements and fashions of thought.[9] In the absence of an adequately articulated and comprehensive *doctrine* on social questions, Catholic thinkers have embraced a spectrum of ideas and positions on politics and economics that have often been in tension with one another or even simply incompatible.[10] An assessment of the Church's formal teaching on social matters over the 135 years or so since Leo XIII's first social encyclical, *Inscrutabili* (1878), will reveal that popes and bishops have, from time to time, felt the need to offer a corrective to the *tradition* when it has drifted too far from a balanced presentation of the Catholic position or when it has tended too far in the direction of adopting a secular philosophy at odds with the Catholic vision of the person and society.[11]

Pontifical Council for Justice and Peace released its unprecedented summary of Catholic social thought, it quite deliberately chose to title it the *Compendium of Catholic Social Doctrine*. This was done purposely to distinguish the *doctrine* of the Church from the vast array of unofficial opinions on social matters that claimed the title "Catholic."

9 Consider an analogy: Catholic social *doctrine* is like a carefully nurtured plant that grows in a rich soil (the *tradition*), a compost of sharp insights, theories in conflict, and thoughtful opinions as well as the lived experience of practical successes and failures. The plant owes a debt to the soil but not everything contained in the soil finds its way into the living roots, stems, leaves, flowers and fruit of the mature plant.

10 The overall project of the popes in this regard has not been to articulate a systematic and complete social doctrine but rather to offer reflections and analysis on contemporary social questions rooted in the Gospel and the Catholic moral tradition. As a result, these reflections appear to some to be what one theologian called "a box of spare parts." But to hold this view is to fail to see the underlying unity rooted in the moral tradition and also to fail to appreciate a sort of authentic development in progress, as the popes attempt over time to be more articulate about the concepts that shape their views.

11 I submit that an example of the former might be Paul VI's insistence on a comprehensive vision of human development in *Populorum progressio* (1967), and examples of the latter may be Cardinal Ratzinger's treatment of human freedom, in *Libertatis nuntius* (1984) and *Libertatis conscientia* (1986), over against some of the tendencies of liberation theology, as well as John Paul II's encyclicals *Veritatis splendor* (1993) and *Evangelium vitae* (1995), which aimed, respectively, to correct discordant ideas in moral theology and in the engagement with culture.

The temptation in the *tradition* to merge secular social theories and Catholic doctrine has seldom been resisted. Secular social theories, which ironically have often drawn their inspiration from a Christian notion of human dignity, , offer a siren's vision of what could be if only the right structures or ordering were set in place. Drawn by the possibilities of improvement, many thinkers try to graft a selection of Catholic ideas on to the main stalk of Socialism, Progressivism, or even Libertarianism.[12]

The Church, however, understands a good society principally in terms of the transcendent destiny of the person. That is to say, a society is good to the degree that it prepares persons to share God's life and love in heaven. A society is not good because it creates (or distributes) a maximum of wealth, unless that creation or distribution promotes holiness. It is not good because it maximizes freedom or equality or any other condition, unless maximizing that condition promotes holiness. By the same token, the mere relief of poverty or hunger or illness, which in the abstract are worthwhile goals, might be undesirable if the means employed also had the effect of undermining holiness.[13] But such a vision can be unpersuasive in a secularized civil society, and so many thinkers are moved to express such Catholic concepts as they can in the language and context of secular theory.

2. A Starting Point: "The glory of God is man fully alive"

The *Compendium* tells us that the "object of the Church's social doctrine is . . . the human person called to salvation."[14] In other words, the goal of the Church's teaching on social issues is to promote the full flourishing and transcendent destiny of the human person. Through the centuries the

---

12 There have been any number of Catholic socialists, including some liberation theologians, whose genuine Catholic compassion led them to see Socialism and the attendant suppression of private property as a means of relieving the distress of the poor. Others, like Msgr. John A. Ryan, who was so influential in American political life in the first half of the twentieth century, sought to unite Catholic ideas with a commitment to Progressive politics. Still others— perhaps Rep. Paul Ryan is one—have found some Catholic principles at least to be congenial to Libertarian ideals.

13 See Paul VI, *Populorum progressio*, no. 18–19.

14 *CSDC* no. 81.

Church has expressed this objective in many ways, from St. Irenaeus's ringing sentence, "The glory of God is man fully alive and the life of man is the vision of God," to Paul VI's focus on "integral human development."[15] Human persons are social in nature, not merely by convenience. As such, we cannot develop and flourish in isolation or in a severely defective society. But the measure of a good society is not conformity to an abstract ideal but the promotion of human well-being in the concrete, which ultimately is the promotion of every aspect of human development and holiness.[16]

For roughly a thousand years, the political organization of Europe remained fairly stable. Communities were organized around both a king or prince and the Church. Christendom was a dynamic union of political and ecclesiastical authorities, often in tension with one another but always conscious that the common faith of the community shaped the whole. As a consequence, the Church came to assume this stability and did not, on a pastoral level, reflect on the fundamental Christian principles that should underlie a good society.[17]

All of this changed very dramatically at the end of the eighteenth century. Pressures that had been slowly building for a century or two were suddenly released in the closing decades of that century and brought about revolutionary changes in the critical dimensions of social life. At first, the Church came under severe attack, particularly in France. Bishops, priests, and religious were arrested and executed. Church property was confiscated and the pastoral work of the Church was severely curtailed and at times

---

15   St. Irenaeus, *Adversus haereses*, IV.20.7; Pope Paul VI, *Populorum progressio*, no. 14–16.

16   Pope Leo XIII, *Sapientiae christianae*, no. 2; *Rerum novarum*, no. 34. Leo XIII's encyclicals were originally published in Latin and without the modern convention of standard paragraph numbers. Nor were official translations provided, as is the norm today. I have followed in this paper the translations and paragraph numbering used by the Vatican website: www.vatican.va.

17   This is not to say that there were no such reflections at all. However, such reflections as did consider matters of principle, usually confined to theologians and canonists, assumed that a monarchical structure would be the norm. Statements from popes and bishops addressing social issues more commonly focused on the continuing tension between civil and ecclesiastical authority, not on the nature of a good society.

prohibited. For decades the assaults continued and most of the Church's attention was directed to defending and preserving what it could, though in the end this proved to be a losing battle. By 1878, when the long pontificate of Pius IX ended and Leo XIII was elected, the Church was facing a set of unprecedented challenges in society.

3. Leo XIII and the Modern Age

During the pontificate of Leo XIII (1878–1903) the Church laid the foundation for an intellectual and pastoral response to the Age of Revolution. In rough outline, the challenge facing Leo—the challenge posed by Liberalism and Socialism—was not how to preserve the position of the Church in society or even simply how to defend Catholic doctrine against new opposition. These were the challenges addressed with limited success by his predecessors. It was instead how to reconceive modern society, in the light of the Gospel, as an organic unity in the face of so many dislocations caused by political, economic, and intellectual revolutions. Whatever problems characterized medieval and early modern societies—and there were many—there was probably a much greater sense of social or cultural unity than in the modern era. Leo's concern was to chart a path toward a social unity (and peace) that could overcome the fractures of modern life without losing the real advantages.

His response, offered in a collection of encyclicals beginning with *Inscrutabili Dei consilio* in 1878 (which letters should not be considered in isolation from one another), was to refresh the foundations of Catholic thought on social matters in order to offer an alternate analysis of modernity. This meant engaging in the analysis through Catholic lenses, not adopting the categories and perspectives of secular theorists.

For some Catholic thinkers, this was precisely what he should not have done. In their view, it was critically necessary that the Church engage modern thought, not by bringing its revitalized tradition to bear but by embracing modernity's premises and accommodating the Church's medieval worldview to new realities.[18] However, Leo believed that it was only by

---

18   The school of thought that came to be called Modernism, represented by thinkers like Loisy and Tyrell, was inclined in this direction.

purifying Catholic thinking, so to speak, that a constructive engagement with modern thought could take place. His project in the social encyclicals (but also in other documents, such as *Aeterni patris* and *Providentissimus Deus*) was to sharpen Catholic intellectual hardware for its engagement with modernity. He was convinced that the premises of modern thought, and the consequent political and economic organization of society, would be disastrous for humanity.[19] Somehow, the message of the Gospel and the vision of the person that followed from it had to be prepared for the encounter.

The social questions at the time thus became: *How can the necessary organic unity be restored to society in the face of the sweeping political, economic, and cultural changes that have occurred? How can a new social order grounded in the Christian vision of the person be set in place that truly instantiates the common good and serves human well-being?* The responses he devised to these questions constituted not so much an alternative to Liberalism and Socialism as a deeper, more comprehensive, and more realistic conception of a good society that continues to serve as a foundation for the Church's social doctrine.

On Leo's view, a good society, the civil community which it is natural for human persons to form, is organic and ordered.[20] As organic, it is not merely a collection or aggregate of individuals, but it is rather a community in which persons play different roles and occupy different places.[21] Some persons may have great talent, energy, or good fortune and come to lead lives of prominence and material comfort. Others may have less talent, less energy, or bad fortune and come to lead lives of poverty. The well-being of the organic community requires the success of the first group but their very success in turn obligates them, sometimes in justice and sometimes in charity, to attend to the needs of those in the second group.[22] The success of such a community as a whole, then, depends upon the mutual respect and

---

19   The violence of the twentieth century and the consequences of the abandonment of hitherto nearly universal moral values (e.g., contraception, abortion, materialism, no-fault divorce, redefinition of marriage, and so on) suggest that Leo was right to be worried.

20   *Quod Apostolici muneris*, no. 5–9.

21   *Rerum novarum*, no. 17, 34; *Graves de communi*, no. 5.

22   *Quod Apostolici muneris*, no. 9; *Rerum novarum*, no. 22.

cooperation of its members. The community prospers in many ways when this cooperation occurs but suffers when cooperation is replaced by conflict.[23]

As a practical matter, Leo accepted the traditional view, endorsed by both Augustine and Aquinas, that, while the structures of society (e.g., laws and customs) are necessary to support the common good, the peace and proper functioning of a community also depend upon the virtue of its members.[24] Law and public authority can only do so much. Personal virtue is indispensable, and indeed the good society is ultimately made good not by its laws and customs but by the virtue of its citizens.[25] Furthermore, the different classes in society need to be mindful of the transcendent destiny of each human person and of the need for each person to develop in virtue.[26]

As an ordered whole, the good society is also hierarchical and structured. It requires the exercise of authority by its very nature, which is a sign that legitimate authority has its origin in God's will.[27] This ordered society also includes within it an array of associations, the most important of which is the family.[28] The state, which is an element of but not the whole of society, is responsible for securing the general conditions that support the good of the whole.[29] However, in the good society these smaller associations attend to a wide variety of human needs and interests, and they

23 *Rerum novarum*, no. 19; *Graves de communi*, no. 8.
24 *Rerum novarum*, no. 28.
25 This view is in sharp opposition to Socialist and Progressive views that maintain that the principal challenge is to change social structures so that the behavior of individuals is forced into new channels that are socially beneficial. Of course, this assumes that these new structures can be designed effectively, that there are indeed experts who are wise enough to engineer society, and that the real challenge is sustaining the political will to implement the changes. For its part, the Church acknowledges that some social structures are toxic and harmful but insists that the solution lies with the personal conversion of citizens, from which structural change will naturally follow. See John Paul II, *Sollicitudo rei socialis*, no. 36.
26 *Rerum novarum*, no. 20.
27 *Inscrutabili dei consilio*, no. 2–6.
28 *Rerum novarum*, no. 13–14.
29 *Quod Apostolici muneris*, no. 6.

do so not by delegation from the state but as a proper function.[30] The state plays its role well if it cultivates these associations and enables them to flourish, but it neither authorizes nor should it absorb their functions. Respect for the variety and proper roles of all these associations is the essence of the principle of subsidiarity.

In sum, the principal duty of the state is to establish and sustain the common good, which in general means that it must attend to those conditions that permit the members of the community to meet their material needs and the needs of their families, to cooperate with one another in their common life, and throughout to exercise their freedom well and to work toward their salvation.[31]

To this end, Leo also insisted on the legitimacy of private ownership as a natural human right. He grounded this right in the duty of parents to care for their families, seeing it not only as a necessary means for securing the material needs of life but also as a defense of individual freedom and a means of guarding individuals and families from changing fortunes.[32] Nevertheless, this right to ownership must always be understood within the context of the common good of society and of the Gospel injunction to charity. The right to be an owner, as natural, cannot be extinguished but it does entail duties and can be regulated by the state.[33] It does not convey an absolute liberty to do as one wishes with one's property.

More concretely, the economic element of the social question that occupied Leo in *Rerum novarum* can be stated as follows: *What private behaviors and public policies are needed to shape the common life of a society so that everyone in the community has a just and reasonable share of material possessions?* Mindful that the Church lacks the expertise to offer detailed technical solutions to such a question, he nevertheless thought it imperative to articulate and explain the principles that should underlie any solutions that would be crafted by communities. In doing so, he was in some sense attempting to recover and to refresh older principles that had been distorted by both Liberalism and Socialism.

30 *Quod Apostolici muneris,* no. 6; *Rerum novarum,* no. 51.
31 *Diuturnum,* no. 11; *Immortale dei,* no. 5.
32 *Rerum novarum,* no. 6–8.
33 *Rerum novarum,* no. 22; see also Pius XI, *Quadragesimo anno,* no. 50–51.

In this regard, justice is assuredly the foundation for reconciliation of the different classes in society and the first responsibility of civil authority.[34] However, while justice is necessary for the good society, it is not sufficient. For Leo, the reconstitution of society, the restoration of harmony between classes, and the achievement of prosperity "must chiefly be brought about by the plenteous outpouring of charity."[35] He understood charity as, first of all, a theological virtue by which a person loves God and other persons in whom he sees the image of God. Following the example and command of Christ, this love of God and others naturally results in "spiritual and corporal works."[36] Charity, properly understood, is far from simply giving something to another; it is the indispensable virtue that perfects justice and makes possible the good society.[37]

Unfortunately, Leo was not entirely successful in his project to respond to Liberalism and Socialism. He did mark out the Church's position on some critical questions, and he did inspire a number of Catholic thinkers to devote their attention to this issue. However, many of them, perhaps in an effort to distance themselves from the errors of opposing views, embraced key Liberal or Socialist premises. They worked hard to reconcile these premises with the doctrine of *Rerum novarum* (and later *Quadragesimo anno*) and in so doing gradually shaped a theory of social justice that moved the Catholic social *tradition* in a new direction.

The history of these developments, like the history of many ideas, is quite complex in its details. No one person was responsible for the evolution that occurred, though some played critical and enduring roles. Very few Catholic thinkers wished to place themselves in opposition to *Rerum novarum*, but some firmly believed that certain of Leo's positions were passé and not applicable to the complex industrial societies of the twentieth century. What is true, however, is that in the decades following the encyclical, the realism of Leo, his vision of a limited but essential role for the state, and his emphasis on the necessity of charity faded from view. In place of these, Catholic thinkers embraced the view that social structures

34 *Rerum novarum*, no. 32–34.
35 *Rerum novarum*, no. 63.
36 *Graves de communi*, no. 15.
37 *Graves de communi*, no. 13.

could be, and must be, engineered and that the dominant goal of action in society was the establishment of a right ordering of these structures, which ordering would constitute a sort of abstract justice. In consequence, a new concept of "social justice" took on a meaning and a preeminence in the tradition that Leo could not have anticipated and likely would not have endorsed.

4. The Concept of "Social Justice"

The idea of social justice, which in many contexts has become synonymous with the Catholic social tradition, is commonly thought to be the principal objective of Catholic action in the public sphere. While a concern for justice has certainly been a part of the thought and action of the Church from its origins, the modern notion of social justice has taken on new meanings and a dominant emphasis in Catholic thinking about social issues. Without diminishing a proper concern for pursuing and securing justice in the world, it is nevertheless necessary to balance a concern for justice with other principles of action. Indeed, it is necessary to define what we understand by justice, particularly social justice, before we can act to secure it.

Like many words in the domains of moral philosophy and theology, "justice" has numerous shades of meaning. In the classical tradition, justice is one of the cardinal virtues. The well-known ancient definition comes from Ulpian: "Justice is the habit by which a man gives to every person, by a constant and perpetual will, what is due to that person."[38] The just person has a permanent disposition to give to others what belongs to them, and this disposition enables him to determine, as far as it may be done, what approximately is just in concrete circumstances. Indeed, on Aristotle's account, the measure of justice in practice is what the truly just person would do.

But "justice" may also refer to a quality of acts, as when we say that a particular choice would be just or unjust. The concept of justice here serves as a sort of measure against which we can judge concrete actions, practices, or policies to be good or bad. We should note that it is always persons who have obligations or duties of justice, never abstract entities like organizations

---

38   Quoted, for example, by St. Thomas Aquinas, *Summa Theologiae*, q. 58, art. 1.

or societies.[39] With regard to the meaning of justice, Aquinas elaborated on the analysis of Aristotle to explain an ordering of different "parts" of the virtue. He went on to distinguish several different kinds.[40] This schema has become an enduring feature of the Catholic moral tradition.

First, he observed that an individual may have obligations either to the community as a whole or to other specific private individuals. The first set of obligations are measured by what he calls *general* justice, or justice owed to the whole. The second set of obligations fall under *particular* justice, or justice owed to parts of the whole (that is, other individuals or groups of individuals). Second, he divided particular justice into two further kinds. One is *commutative* justice, which measures the right relationship between equals. Commutative justice demands equality in transactions (for example, receiving a fair price for an item sold) or restitution (compensation for a harm done to another).

The second kind of particular justice is what Aquinas called *distributive*. This is much misunderstood today but the basic idea is fairly simple and part of our common experience. Whereas commutative justice describes the duty of a private individual or group to other private individuals or groups, distributive justice describes the duty of an individual acting on behalf of a group (such as a family, an organization, or a society) with regard to members of the group. It measures the actions of such an individual in distributing the benefits, honors, and burdens that belong to the community to its members. For example, the leader of a community is bound by distributive justice in providing, say, welfare benefits or support for education, or in determining tax rates or who must serve on a jury.

Whereas commutative justice requires people to be treated equally regardless of their personal characteristics, distributive justice requires that

---

39 On the classic analysis, when we say that an organization or a society has a duty, what we really mean is that the individuals responsible for determining the organization's actions, the leaders of the organization, are the ones who have the duty.

40 A classic treatment of justice in Aquinas is Josef Pieper, *Justice* (New York: Pantheon, 1955). A fine brief treatment can be found in Thomas Gilby, Principality and Polity (London: Longman Greens and Co., 1958) 208-227. Both writers, however, are not as clear as they might be about the nature of general justice.

the leader consider relevant personal characteristics. For example, if a provision is made to provide a grant for higher education out of community funds, it is not given in equal amounts to everyone in the community. It is given to people who are qualified to receive a higher education, who are actually pursuing such an education, and who have a particular need for community assistance.

A common misunderstanding arises here. Distributive justice, in the classic account that is part of the Church's heritage of moral theology, does not entail or empower the leaders of a political community to confiscate private property from those who have much in order to distribute it to those who have less. Strictly speaking, distributive justice always assumes that what is distributed is a common possession of the community. The state may have valid reasons, and its leaders may act rightly, to take private property on occasion for a legitimate public purpose.[41] Ordinarily, the state then would have a duty to compensate the owners for what it had taken (a sort of commutative justice). The state might also have a differential system of taxation, by which it demanded proportionately more from individuals with higher incomes or greater wealth to support its legitimate activities (a sort of distributive justice, properly considered). But simply transferring wealth from one private individual to another is not considered by the tradition to be a matter of distributive justice.

Returning to the idea of general justice, Aquinas also divides this into two forms. The object of the first form is the common good in general, as distinct from a persons or a determinate group of persons who could be identified. As a virtue, this consists in the habitual inclination to support the common good of the society as occasions arise to do so. One might think of ordinary people who spontaneously come to the aid of disaster victims as exhibiting this form of justice or of business people who are alert to the ways in which they might serve otherwise neglected members of the community.

The object of the second form of general justice is the law, and Aquinas speaks of this as legal justice. This form of justice principally resides in civil

---

41   The state certainly has the authority to confiscate private property that was unjustly taken from its proper owners (whether through theft, fraud or other means) with a view to restoring it to those from whom it was taken. Ordinarily, however, this would be a matter of commutative justice.

authorities charged with enacting laws for the community, who are bound to devise specific ways in which the common good is to be served. Good laws must accord with the natural law, must promote the common good, and ought to make reasonable accommodations to the culture of the society. (Laws that demand a level of virtue that people do not possess or that ask less of them than they are capable of doing, fail in this last respect.) Here one might imagine anything from traffic laws to laws regulating markets to tax levies.

But what should we make of "social justice"? Where does this fit in the classic schema? The answer is that it depends upon context. On the secular side, beginning roughly in the middle of the 19th century, philosophers, economists and sociologists in the Anglo-American scholarly world began to promote a reconsideration of the idea of justice. They offered the phrase "social justice" as an alternative to the older analysis, which they sometimes called "personal," "civic" or "political" justice. What they had in mind, more or less, was a situation in society in which the aggregate wealth of the community was distributed more reasonably according to, say, productivity or need.[42] Or, more generally, in an oft-quoted definition: [Social justice is achieved with] the satisfaction of everyone's wants so far as they are not outweighed by others' wants."[43] In a subtle shift, the idea of justice has been changed from a virtue of persons to a set of preferred outcomes and ultimately to an ensemble of structures, expertly devised and firmly imposed, that would ensure these outcomes.[44]

On the other hand, the phrase entered the papal literature most prominently with the publication by Pius XI of the encyclical *Quadragesimo anno* in 1931. The term had been used somewhat casually and without precise

---

42 For example, Thomas Nixon Carver, *Essays in Social Justice* (Cambridge, MA: Harvard University Press, 1915), pp 130-131, where he favors a "democratic or liberalistic theory" of distribution "according to productivity, usefulness or worth."

43 One searches in vain among Progressive writers of this era for a formal definition of social justice. This sentence comes closer than most. It is attributed to Lester F Ward by Roscoe Pound in his presidential address to the American Bar Association, *Annual Report of the American Bar Association*, 30 (1907) 911-926, at 921. However, I have not found these words in Ward's text, though they are consistent with his thought.

44 Lester F Ward, *Applied Sociology* (Boston: The Athenaeum Press, 1906), pp 24–25.

definition by a handful of European theologians in the nineteenth century.[45] Without drawing explicitly on these earlier discussions, Pius introduced the phrase and employed it eight times in the encyclical, in all but one case coupled with the terms "common good" or "social charity."[46] It is useful to recall that at the time the encyclical was being prepared, the industrialized world was coping with the early stages of the Great Depression. Pius' text reflects the common view of the time that business leaders wielded great economic power which they often used to appropriate unfair advantages to themselves and to suppress the legitimate demands of workers. The back-drop to all eight of his uses of the term "social justice" is this conviction that the social order will remain gravely wounded as long as those who are powerful act to distort the economic system to their own ends. He appeals to them to act justly, that is, to act in support of the health of the commu-nity as a whole and in particular to ensure that workers receive a just share of the profits of the companies for which they labor.[47]

What precisely does "social justice" mean here? It would be no exaggeration to say that this question was hotly debated by theologians for several decades following the publication of the encyclical.[48] Was Pius using this phrase in a general and non-technical sense? Did he have in mind a specification of the

---

45   See Normand J. Paulhus, "Uses and Misuses of the Term 'Social Justice' in the Roman Catholic Tradition," *Journal of Religious Ethics* 15 (1987), 261–82, for a brief discussion of some of these early uses. Careful scholars also note that the phrase had sometimes previously been used by Pius XI and his pre-decessors in rather vague ways. *Quadragesimo anno* marks the first time that the phrase was used as an important element of a papal encyclical, though still somewhat loosely.

46   See *Quadragesimo anno*, no. 57–58, 71, 74, 88, 101, 110, and 126.

47   It is interesting, but rarely observed, that Pius issued a very brief encyclical addressing the misery of the Depression less than six months after *Quadrage-simo anno* was published. In this encyclical, *Nova impendet* (2 October 1931), Pius appealed to Catholics everywhere to launch a "crusade of charity" to re-lieve the suffering of those in poverty. He clearly hoped for and anticipated countless acts of private generosity; he did not call for government action to address the situation, which he described in the most urgent terms.

48   For example, no fewer than three doctoral dissertations on this question were written in the United States in 1941, the 50th anniversary of *Rerum novarum* and a decade after *Quadragesimo anno*. See William Ferree, *The Act of Social*

classic forms of justice attuned to the new realities of the twentieth century? Or was he, perhaps, defining an altogether new species of justice? And if so, how would this new species relate to the traditional analysis of justice?[49] While there has been continued discussion about the proper meaning of "social justice," there has simply been no common agreement among theologians on this question.[50] However, Jean-Ives Calvez and Jacques Perrin, in two appendices to a highly-regarded study of papal social teaching, concluded that the term "social justice" should be understood as a synonym of Aquinas's general justice.[51]

Justice (Washington, D.C.: Catholic University of America Press, 1942); Leo W. Shields, *The History and Meaning of the Term "Social Justice"* (Notre Dame, IN: University of Notre Dame, 1941); and Thomas E. Henneberry, *On Definitions of Social Justice* (Woodstock College, 1941).

49 The questions were further complicated by Pius' use of the phrase in a later encyclical, *Divini redemptoris* (1937), the general focus of which was the threat posed by Communism. In two places in this encyclical (which is often overlooked by those who later debated the meaning he intended for "social justice") he uses the phrase either to mean the right ordering of society, synonymous with the common good (no. 31), or else as a synonym for the classic concept of legal justice (no. 52).

50 It is not my intention here to summarize a complicated discussion pursued for eight decades or more. In addition to the essay by Paulhus and the dissertations cited in the earlier notes, the interested reader may also consult some of the following: William Ferree, *Introduction to Social Justice* (New York: Paulist Press, 1948); William F. Drummond, S.J., *Social Justice* (Milwaukee, WI: Bruce Publishing, 1955); Raymond Jancauskas, S.J., "The Concept of Social Justice: Some Current Applications," *Review of Social Economy* 17 (1959), 34–50; Jean-Yves Calvez and Jacques Perrin, *The Church and Social Justice* (Chicago: Regnery, 1961), especially chapters 6 and 7; David Hollenbach, S.J., "Modern Catholic Teachings Concerning Justice," in John C Haughey, S.J., ed., *The Faith that Does Justice* (New York: Paulist Press, 1977), 207–31; J. Brian Benestad, "The Catholic Concept of Social Justice: A Historical Perspective," *Communio* 11 (1984), 365–81; Carl L. Bankston III, "Social Justice: Cultural Origins of a Perspective and a Theory," *The Independent Review* 15 (2010), 165–78 (Bankston provides a sociologist's perspective on some of the later developments in secular thinking about social justice); Edward J. O'Boyle, "Social Justice: Addressing the Ambiguity," *Logos* 14 (2011), 96–117.

51 Jean-Ives Calvez and Jacques Perrin, *Église et société économique* (Paris: Éditions Montaigne, 1959). Curiously, the English translation, *The Church and Social Justice*, entirely omits these appendices.

There are at least two reasons for this confusion in the modern Catholic tradition. One is that the Church, in its formal documents on social issues, still prefers not to offer precise definitions for the terms it uses and continues to use a number of key terms loosely.[52] This persistent vagueness in papal expressions opened the door to a second factor.

A number of twentieth-century Catholic thinkers in this arena have often been strongly influenced by secular social theories, particularly Progressivism, and somewhat indirectly by the ideas promoted by the Protestant Social Gospel movement. These schools of thought put some flesh on the skeleton of Catholic social tradition, and encouraged not only a focus on government as the locus of work for social justice but also the conviction that the desired objectives can be achieved by an expert restructuring of society (brought about by enlightened government action).

5. The Evolution of the Idea of Social Justice

In what follows, I will try to describe the effect of these factors on the evolution of the concept of social justice in three rough stages. I want to emphasize that I regard this to be an evolution in the *tradition*, not the *doctrine*, of the Church, but it is the tradition that has now become the lens through which the doctrine is communicated and understood.[53] This helps to explain why Benedict XVI felt the need to offer a corrective to this evolution in his two social encyclicals, as we shall see.

Leo XIII did not use the term "social justice" in his published work, though the phrase had some modest currency in nineteenth-century Italy. Despite the controversy surrounding Pius XI's introduction of the term in

52 For example, both the *Catechism of the Catholic Church* and the *Compendium of the Social Doctrine of the Church* use the phrase "social justice" a number of times, but neither document offers a precise definition of what it means by the term. Particular uses are often quite generic and not helpful for fixing a clear meaning.

53 Needless to say, this description of the evolution of social justice will be somewhat general and imprecise. No one author fully exemplifies the changes and therefore I can do little more here than offer some illustrations in lieu of proof. I realize that this leaves my account open to criticism but I will leave it to the reader to decide if it seems reasonable and rings true.

Quadragesimo anno, it is quite plausible to conclude, as many later commentators did, that he had something in mind that was very close to the classical understanding of legal justice. Indeed, he defined it in this way quite precisely in a later encyclical.[54] And the phrases "legal justice" or "common good" could be substituted for every use of "social justice" in *Quadragesimo anno* without loss of meaning.

Nevertheless, a number of Catholic thinkers in the 1930s began to see in the term "social justice" a new idea in the teaching of the Church. One was Msgr. John A. Ryan, the most prominent American Catholic public theologian of the first half of the twentieth century.[55] Ryan, who was a protégé of Archbishop Ireland of St. Paul, began his academic career with a doctoral dissertation at the Catholic University on the concept of a living wage, a very unusual topic for a theologian to choose in 1905. Even more unusual was Ryan's dedication of the published version of his dissertation to Richard Ely, perhaps the foremost Progressive economist of the day. While Ryan was well versed in classical moral theology, he was also deeply influenced by the Progressive movement and his work often reflects his determination to merge the two schools of thought. Following the publication of *Quadragesimo anno* in 1931, Ryan dedicated himself to developing a vision of social justice that was both Catholic and Progressive.

Ryan affirmed Leo's commitment to the right of ownership as well as the attendant duties of stewardship. However, drawing on, but moving beyond, Pius XI's discussion of superfluous wealth,[56] Ryan favored government action to limit personal incomes, the accumulation of wealth, and the conveyance of wealth through inheritance.[57] Where the tradition had long

---

54 Pius XI, *Divini redemptoris*, no. 51.

55 For much of his career, Ryan (1869–1945) was a professor at the Catholic University of America, but he was also instrumental in the formation of the National Catholic Welfare Conference. For some twenty years he was head of the Social Action Department of the Conference, in which capacity he was a trusted advisor to bishops, Congress, and even President Roosevelt. A prolific writer, Ryan did more than any other Catholic theologian in America to increase awareness of the Church's social tradition.

56 *Quadragesimo anno*, no. 50–51.

57 John A. Ryan, "The Legal Limitation of Fortunes," in *Distributive Justice*, 3d edition (New York: Macmillan, 1942), 223–32.

insisted that the right of ownership was qualified by the urgent need of others for the necessities of life, Ryan thought that the right to own superfluous wealth or to receive excessive income was also qualified by the need to establish right order in society.[58] Social justice, on his view, went beyond legal justice to entail this sort of redistribution: "Inasmuch as 'social justice' comprises the common good, it is the same as legal justice; inasmuch as it requires society to bring about a proper distribution of goods among all classes, it comprises distributive justice."[59] Second, Ryan was deeply persuaded of the Progressive view that the insights of the social sciences, including economics, sociology, and management, could design social structures that would effectively instantiate the common good, in spite of or perhaps even in opposition to the resistance of the wealthy and powerful. To his credit, he had great sympathy for the poor and the working class and spent much of his life in the effort to improve their situation. His focus was principally on the goal of setting in place a just distribution of the national income.[60] In pursuing this goal, however, he favored a subtle difference from Leo's vision. Leo had imagined a reordering of society that would create the conditions favorable to a desirable distribution of income and wealth as a result of the free collaboration of workers and owners, inspired by justice and charity. The role of the state in this vision was essentially to establish and protect these conditions (and perhaps in cases of necessity to provide direct relief to the needy). Ryan, on the other hand, sought not merely to establish the conditions for fruitful collaboration but to ensure, by other means as necessary, the distribution of income that ought to have been the goal of such collaboration. In other words, where Leo thought that class hostility could be

58 "The Duty of Distributing Superfluous Wealth," in *Distributive Justice*, 3d edition (New York: Macmillan, 1942), 233–45. It should be added that Ryan thought that an objective measure of "superfluous wealth" or "excessive income" was available and could be employed by public authorities in pursuit of a just social order.

59 John A. Ryan, "The Concept of Social Justice," *The Catholic Charities Review*, vol. 18 (December 1934), 314.

60 *Distributive Justice*, 3–4. Ryan comes close to construing the economist's abstract measure of national income, the sum of all income received by individuals in the nation, to be a real public good which could not be fairly distributed by the vagaries of the marketplace.

overcome and collaboration successful, Ryan held that external controls were necessary, and morally justified, to ensure a successful outcome.

While Ryan did not subscribe to the Socialist conviction that class conflict was inevitable, neither was he as confident as Leo had been that the tension between workers and owners could be overcome without external pressure. Perhaps an additional forty or fifty years of experience with industrial organizations and labor unions had persuaded him that the collaboration would require external incentives, both positive and negative.

As a consequence, Ryan favored a rather different role for the state from Leo and probably from Pius. For a variety of reasons, not least of which was the Church's experience with a number of oppressive governments in the nineteenth century, Leo was skeptical about expanding the role of the state.[61] To be sure, he insisted that the state had an important role to play in the economic affairs of the community, but he also understood that the society is more than the state. Some critical aspects of the life of society could and should be managed by citizens themselves without direction by the state. Pius seems to have accepted this view in large part, though he also recognized that the increased complexity of social life could require more attention from civil authorities. Even so, he had his own reasons, given the Church's experience of the Fascism of Mussolini, to be cautious about relying on the state to achieve social justice.

As a Progressive, however, Ryan was committed to the view that government could be an impartial and clear-eyed judge of the regulations and policies needed to secure the common good. This entailed for him the conviction that the agents of government, as social science professionals, could be more or less immune to pressure from special interests and that they could understand enough about society and human behavior to craft and implement policies that would really achieve the desired ends.

---

61 No doubt the differences in judgments between Leo and Ryan arose partly from their differences in experiences. Where European governments—French, Italian, Austrian, German—tended in the nineteenth century to be heavy-handed and certainly oppressive where the Church was concerned, the American experience of government was quite different. Many Americans, though certainly not all, had come to consider the federal government an honest proponent of the national welfare. It is interesting to imagine what these two might make of national governments in America and Europe today.

As a theologian, Ryan was not dismissive of charity, and he understood what it meant as a theological virtue. However, he tended to see charity as related to the actual and local distribution of wealth rather than a foundation for the reordering of society. For example, he could consider the distribution of superfluous wealth as an obligation either of justice or of charity, as long as it was recognized as an obligation.[62] The right ordering of society was something else.

Finally, as a priest, the importance of the transcendent destiny of individuals was hardly lost on Ryan, but in his work on economic issues it did not play a significant role. On one level, this is not surprising, as Ryan was writing for a non-theological audience and was not writing as a pastor. On another level, though, and however unintentionally, he provided a model for theologians to compartmentalize the evaluation of moral issues, to consider issues as political questions of justice and not as issues with wider theological meaning.

The work of Ryan and his colleagues served as a foundation for Catholic thinkers in the 1940s and 1950s, but many of these thinkers moved on to appropriate not only secular political theories but also philosophical and theological concepts from outside the Catholic tradition. The third stage, which for lack of a better name we might call the *Modern Catholic Vision* of social justice, has been strongly represented in America and throughout the world from the 1960s to the present. In many Catholic circles it has become the default mode of thinking on the subject, though there are indications that it may now be on the wane.

The Modern Catholic Vision is less systematic and more diffuse and so quite impossible to attribute a single individual. Nevertheless, certain key elements can be crystallized, so to speak, even if no single writer clearly presents every element.

First, while the right to own property privately ought to be respected (as against the Socialists), in practice this right is subordinated to the right of all members of the community to have a minimally fair share of the goods of creation.[63] Where Leo and Ryan were inclined to say that,

---

62 *Distributive Justice*, 234–35.
63 "Social justice can, therefore, be defined as a special species of justice, distinct from commutative, legal, and distributive, which requires that material goods,

in ordinary circumstances, an individual's right to the necessities of life was activated by his work, the Modern Catholic Vision sees this right as a claim on society directly, and not necessarily a result of one's active participation in the production of these public goods.[64] Private ownership is contingent upon society fulfilling its obligation to ensure this minimum fair share.

But the difference does not end here. Where Leo and Ryan conceived of the distribution of the material necessities of life, this Modern Catholic Vision entails a wide range—potentially unlimited—of human goods, which might include education, cultural participation, medical care, access to information and communication technologies, and so on.[65] While there are many dimensions to human fulfillment, the potential demands on society imagined by this view bring us into an entirely new realm.

In combination, the emphasis on the individual's right to claim goods from society and the expansion of the goods to be considered relevant has moved proponents of the Modern Catholic Vision to expand greatly the notion of public goods. For example, where an earlier vision of the common good might have seen, say, medical care as a good for human persons, it

even privately owned, shall serve the common use of all men." William F. Drummond, S.J., *Social Justice* (Milwaukee: Bruce Publishing, 1955), 55.

64   "Even though participation in the creation of these public goods may be minimal, or, in the case of children, infirm or aged persons, presently non-existent, the tradition claims that membership in the human community creates a bond between persons sufficient to ground a right for all to share in the public good to the minimum degree compatible with human dignity. Distributive justice thus is the norm which states the obligation of society and the state to guarantee this participation by all in the common good." David Hollenbach, S.J., "Modern Catholic Teachings Concerning Justice," in John C. Haughey, S.J., ed., *The Faith that Does Justice* (New York: Paulist Press, 1977), 220.

65   "Distributive justice specifies the claim which all persons have to some share in those goods which are essentially public or social. Such goods as the fertility of the earth, the productivity of an industrialized economy and the security provided by advanced systems of health care and social insurance are seen by the documents of the tradition as products of the social system as a whole." David Hollenbach, S.J., "Modern Catholic Teachings Concerning Justice," in John C. Haughey, S.J., ed., *The Faith that Does Justice* (New York: Paulist Press, 1977), 219.

also understood this good to be largely provided by private transactions between physician and patient. The role of public authority would have been to remove obstacles that would have made it difficult for persons to receive medical care, but public authority had no obligation to provide it.[66] Indeed, the provision of medical care to the poor has been an outstanding element of the charitable work of the Church, and properly so. By contrast, the Modern Catholic Vision is inclined to see medical care as a public good, i.e., as a common possession of the community, and so subject to distributive justice, administered by public authority.[67]

Second, this vision of social justice understands the objective to be the reordering of society so that a set of new structures (laws, regulations, policies, and practices) is put in place that will ensure a desirable distribution of public goods.[68] The goal is no longer, as it was for Leo, establishing conditions which make it possible for people to collaborate and achieve the common good; it is now devising and implementing structures that *ensure* the material distribution that Leo's common good was to facilitate.

66 The state at one level or another now so commonly provides both medical care and education that we have come to assume that it has always been so. However, until the nineteenth century both education and medical care were ordinarily private matters. Many religious orders, especially communities of women, came into being in the seventeenth and eighteenth centuries precisely to serve these needs.

67 "Social injustice cannot be solved by individuals, private organizations, businesses, or the government alone. The participation of each is necessary but not sufficient. . . . The formal organizing element of society, the government, or the state has a significant but not exclusive responsibility to address these concerns [injustice]. . . . Social justice takes precedence over other forms of justice. . . . Social justice then is the responsibility of all (including the vulnerable) to promote the well-being of the vulnerable (for example, the powerless, poor, sick, aged, children) particularly through the critique of established social structures and social institutions." Bernard V. Brady, *The Moral Bond of Community* (Washington, D.C.: Georgetown University Press, 1998), 122.

68 ". . . [Since] social justice is concerned with ordering the activity of individuals and groups to produce the common good, its content is defined in terms of institutional structures, especially with deployment of institutional power in society." David Hollenbach, S.J., *Claims in Conflict* (New York: Paulist Press, 1979), 153.

This difference between conditions that support human flourishing and the realization of a desired level of distribution is quite significant. For one thing, it assumes (perhaps counter to fact) that one can actually know what structures will produce the desired effect. It is at least true that no society has yet achieved this. There is also an unresolved issue of costs, not merely material costs but the potential sacrifice of freedom that might be demanded, and the assault on human dignity that this would entail. Finally, there is arguably a confusion here between what is achievable in the City of Man and what is promised in the City of God. Pointing to a biblical and prophetic model of justice for the City of Man, to be established not by conversion and personal virtue but by structural renewal, is quite a departure from the realism of Leo XIII.[69]

Furthermore, it tends strongly to the ideal. That is, a society is unjust to the degree that it falls short of an ideal distribution of all of the appropriate goods. Where Leo quite freely acknowledged the practical limitations of a fallen world, and even Ryan admitted limits to what could reasonably be accomplished, this later vision tends to be in pursuit of a retreating horizon.

And perhaps because of the persistent difficulty in achieving its ideal, the Modern Catholic Vision tends to see work for social justice to be a struggle against opponents of the poor and the working class. This encourages the very notion of class conflict that Leo and Pius were so concerned to diminish.

The Modern Catholic Vision also acknowledges a much larger role for the state in the pursuit of the common good. Action for social justice is seen principally to be action to encourage public authorities to pass legislation and regulations, to appropriate funds, and generally to set in place structures that proponents believe will ensure the outcomes they desire.[70]

---

69 See, for example, the U.S. Bishops' pastoral letter, *Economic Justice for All* (1986) and Fred Kammer, S.J., *Doing Faithjustice* (Mahwah, NJ: Paulist Press, 1991).

70 "Distributive justice orders the exercise of competing rights claims in such a way that no one (or at least a minimum number of persons) is excluded from participation in those goods which are essentially social. Furthermore, the entire society is under obligation to create institutions which make the satisfaction of these demands of distributive justice possible. This demand is met

For this reason, they tend to invert the role of charity. On their view, charity may be a motivation for Christians to pursue the larger work of social justice, or it may be a local act of immediate relief, with the larger work of addressing the causes of distress left to the pursuit of social justice.[71]

As powerful as the Modern Catholic Vision has been in recent decades, there are signs that its influence may be declining. The measures of progress that we might have hoped to see achieved have not been met. Poverty rates have not declined, family stability is far worse, unemployment and underemployment have not abated, and so on. At the same time, federal, state, and local deficits have soared. Some bishops have begun to wonder aloud about the justice of imposing such costs on succeeding generations and about the practical limitations of social reordering driven by government action rather than personal conversion and cultural change. More recently, given the pressures on free exercise of religion imposed by federal and state governments (e.g., health care mandates, redefinitions of marriage), bishops have become more skeptical about the decades-long policies of lobbying government to produce social reform. Perhaps the time has come for an alternative.

6. The Recovery of Charity

As a practical matter, an honest observer would have to admit that the social difficulties identified by Leo XIII in 1891, and affirmed by Pius XI in 1931, have not disappeared today. Indeed, every pope from Pius XII to Francis has acknowledged that the common good (i.e., social justice) has not been

---

through the society acting in a politically organized way—that is, through government. Social justice, therefore, is the ordering of rights through legislation and other forms of government activity." David Hollenbach, S.J., *Claims in Conflict* (New York: Paulist Press, 1979), 155.

71 "A common distinction made between charity and justice is to see the former as addressing immediate need through direct aid while the latter looks at longer-term solutions through social analysis and change. Another way of putting it is to see charity as a response to the *effects* of personal and social ills while justice aims at remedying the *causes* of such ills." Kenneth R. Himes, O.F.M., *Responses to 101 Questions on Catholic Social Teaching* (New York: Paulist Press, 2001), 45.

established. Perhaps progress has been made in some respects—the situation of workers in developed countries is better in many ways than it was a century ago—but much remains to be done. It may be that the opponents of justice are too strong or that advocates for justice have not done enough, or it may be that another element is missing.

I suggest that another element is indeed missing and that the Modern Catholic Vision concerning social justice has systematically neglected something that the popes have consistently taught is indispensable for the development of a good society. This element is charity. I submit that the emphasis that Pope Benedict has given to charity in his two social encyclicals constitutes his effort to restore charity to its proper place of primacy in Catholic social doctrine.

The nature of charity

As noted above, charity is often misunderstood to be nothing more than the act of gratuitously relieving the need or suffering of another. Considered in this sense, and following a Marxist analysis, charity is sometimes seen as an obstacle to establishing justice in society since the aid offered by charity diminishes the pain of injustice and so reduces the motivation for change.[72] Even if they do not share this judgment, some Christians do see charitable efforts as a distraction from the more fundamental task of changing social structures. However, this is neither a proper understanding of charity nor, according to Catholic social doctrine, a proper analysis of the relationship between charity and social justice.

Most properly, charity in the Catholic moral tradition is understood to be a theological virtue, which is a supernatural habit by which persons love God and other human beings, in whom they recognize an image of the God they love. This love naturally results in a profound determination to serve the well-being of the other, whether or not one has strict obligations in justice to the other. The variety of services that the Church has historically provided to the needy are effects of charity, not charity itself. Nevertheless, the ministries of charity are essential to the life of the Church and not a contingent element of the Church's activity in the world.[73]

72 Benedict XVI, *Deus caritas est*, no. 26, 31.
73 *Deus caritas est*, no. 25.

These ministries, furthermore, must be informed by the truth about the human person, not least by the fact of his transcendent destiny.[74] This truth about the person sets practical activities in perspective, whether they are aimed at immediate relief of distress or at structural reform. Love of the other that seeks the good of the other is misplaced if what truly constitutes the good of the other is not clearly understood. In this regard, man's material welfare is only one component, and not the most important component, of the good for human persons. And it is through the lens of charity that we come to understand the most profound truths about human persons.[75]

Charity as the foundation of Catholic social doctrine

"Charity is at the heart of the Church's social doctrine. Every responsibility and every commitment spelled out by that doctrine is derived from charity." So wrote Pope Benedict XVI at the beginning of his encyclical *Caritas in veritate*.[76] "Charity in truth . . . is the principal driving force behind the authentic development of every person and of all humanity."[77]

If truth were told, none of us wants to live in a perfectly just world, for in such a world we would each receive precisely what we deserve. In truth, each of us wishes to live in a merciful world, in which our mistakes and sins are forgiven and overlooked, in which second and third chances are readily available, in which undeserved help is offered where needed. It is charity, not justice, that is the foundational value in such a world. It is charity, not justice, that makes life in society truly humane.[78]

The Church's social doctrine begins not in the recognition of injustice, which is a universal experience in human society, but in the recognition, most clearly evidenced in the ministry of Jesus, that each of us is the subject of God's merciful love. Seeing in the other the dignity that prompted this merciful love, injustices done to this other become intolerable and must be

---

74 Benedict XVI, *Caritas in veritate*, no. 1–4.

75 *Caritas in veritate*, no. 2.

76 *Caritas in veritate*, no. 2.

77 *Caritas in veritate*, no. 1.

78 John Paul II, *Dives in misericordia*, no. 14: "Only love (including that kindly love we call 'mercy') is capable of restoring man to himself."

remedied, first in an immediate response to relieve distress and then in action to improve society. Charity makes action in society personal. It does not permit the search for justice to become a quest for an abstract social order in which the consequences for individuals become unimportant and unnoticed.[79]

Charity as distinctive of Christian witness and action in the world

"For the Church, charity is not a kind of welfare activity which could equally well be left to others but is a part of her nature, an indispensable expression of her very being."[80] The distinctive characteristic of Christian action in the world is the manifestation of charity, "making present here and now the love which man always needs."[81]

Benedict emphasized the fact that this manifestation of charity is the special gift that the Christian brings to activities to address the needs of others. "The need for a service of love," he wrote, can never be eliminated. "Whoever wants to eliminate love is preparing to eliminate man as such."[82] In other words, the material needs of the person, however important and urgent they may be, are not all that the person needs. And even supplying these needs in abundance can fail to affirm the dignity of the person if charity is absent. Christian service, animated by the whole truth about human dignity, is a persistent witness to the irreducible value and transcendent destiny of each person.

Charity and Justice

Each pope, from Leo XIII to Francis, who has addressed the question of justice in society has also emphasized the importance of charity and mercy.[83] The need for charity emerges on several levels. Counterintuitive

---

79   The twentieth century was the worst of all eras for this, in which millions of lives were sacrificed—in Germany, in the Soviet Union, in China, in Cambodia, and elsewhere—in pursuit of abstract social orderings, common goods without charity.

80   *Deus caritas est*, no. 25.

81   *Deus caritas est*, no. 31.

82   *Deus caritas est*, no. 28.

83   See, for example, Leo XIII, *Rerum novarum*, no. 63; Pius XI, *Quadragesimo anno*, no. 137; John XXIII, *Mater et magistra*, no. 6, 120; Paul VI, *Octogesima*

as it may seem, as a practical matter, a just society cannot be developed without charity. Charity is not merely an ideal; it is also eminently practical.[84]

As Benedict observed, the establishment of justice in a community is essentially a political task.[85] However, there are several obstacles that lie in the path which may require charity to overcome. The first of these is the very definition of justice in the concrete. It is easy enough to define justice in the abstract, to acknowledge that it requires giving others their due. But in the concrete, in a world of finite resources, special interests and pressures, and conflicting claims, the practical definition of justice is anything but straightforward.

Charity, which impels us to give to the other not only what is his (justice) but also what is ours, opens the possibility of practical solutions to the problem of justice.[86] The complexity of social life means that strict and consistent justice can never really be achieved; justice in practice, in important matters at least, is always a compromise of sorts. Charity, a willingness to accept something less than one might be due in justice, creates openings for practical solutions.

Charity also moves individuals and communities to forgiveness. Forgiveness is never a demand of justice. Indeed, the demand for justice is an impediment to forgiveness. But in a sinful world, everyone is in need of forgiveness and strict justice is practically impossible. Building a just society, as a practical matter, requires both that people in the political process are willing to compromise, to give up something that they might otherwise justly demand, and that they overlook some past offenses in order to achieve what good they can in the present.

---

adveniens, no. 23; John Paul II, *Dives in misericordia*, no. 14; and of course, Benedict XVI, *Deus caritas est* and *Caritas in veritate*.

84 Part of the truth that informs charity has to be the truth about the human person and the human situation, which must include the data of revelation. Without knowing who we are and what we are for, attempts to create a good society cannot succeed. Secular programs, which systematically ignore or reject religious insights, also systematically fail and cannot identify the cause of their failure.

85 *Deus caritas est*, no. 28.

86 *Caritas in veritate*, no. 6.

There are any number of contemporary political situations in which this dynamic plays out. In many cases, justice is impossible and conflict unavoidable because of the unwillingness of parties to give and forgive.[87] The Israeli-Palestinian situation is a prominent example but so also is the controversy about American immigration policy. In the latter case, there are undoubtedly many violations of current law, but there are also problems with the law, to say nothing of economic and social policies and practices that have provoked a movement of peoples. As long as important actors in the political process insist on strict justice, it is unlikely that a satisfactory solution can be found.

Charity not only makes practical justice possible, it also supplements justice. Justice on its own is inadequate. Benedict XVI, echoing the judgment of Pius XI, wrote eloquently about the limitations of justice.[88] We might note here two of his observations. First, justice and charity are not alternatives. There can be no charity without justice; we cannot give to the other what is ours if we are not willing first to give him what is his. In this regard, charity can never be a condescension in which a superior bestows something undeserved upon an inferior. Charity may give beyond the demands of justice but in doing so it recognizes the worth of the other and the fact that both giver and receiver are subjects of the merciful love of God.

Second, "there is no ordering of the state so just that it can eliminate the need for a service of love." There is a human need for love that can be addressed not by rightly ordered social structures but only by a ministry of charity. To think that charity is superfluous or merely a temporary measure of relief while just social structures are devised and set in place "masks a materialist conception of man."

In the Catholic vision, in one respect, justice and charity are complementary. While it is possible to distinguish them in the abstract, in the

---

87 "Charity transcends justice and completes it in the logic of giving and forgiving. The earthly city is promoted not merely by relationships of rights and duties but to an even greater and more fundamental extent by relationships of gratuitousness, mercy and communion." Benedict XVI, *Caritas in veritate*, no. 6. See also no. 4: Charity "is not merely useful but essential for building a good society."

88 *Deus caritas est*, no. 28.

concrete one cannot be present without the other. In another respect, however, charity is the foundation of Catholic social doctrine. It addresses a deeper need of the person, it makes possible the achievement of justice in many ways, and it points to the transcendent destiny and ultimate value of each person.

However we define social justice, therefore, and however important it may be as an objective, it cannot be separated from charity, properly understood. The emphasis on social justice in the Catholic social *tradition* during the twentieth century has tended to lose sight of this, even though popes have frequently made the observation. One consequence of this has been the evolution—one might even say distortion—of a particular concept of social justice and the embrace of this concept as if it were the core of Catholic social *doctrine*. The social encyclicals of Benedict XVI constitute a powerful corrective to the tradition in this regard as well as an articulate statement of and development of the social doctrine of the Church. When considered in this light, which echoes virtually every pope from Leo XIII to John Paul II, the irreplaceable and ultimate foundation of a good society is not justice (which is necessary but insufficient) but charity.

Chapter Seven

The USCCB Approach to Social Justice and the Common Good

J. Brian Benestad
Assumption College

Anyone following the political statements of the variously named episcopal conferences of the U.S. bishops from the late 1960s until the present time knows that they have regularly issued policy statements on matters pertaining to the defense of life (especially the unborn), family life, social justice, and global solidarity. From 1966 until July 1, 2001, the bishops called themselves the National Conference of Catholic bishops (NCCB) and the United States Catholic Conference (USCC). At that point they renamed themselves the United States Conference of Catholic Bishops (USCCB).

Closer students of the USCCB notice that most of its statements on social justice are not matters of faith and morals but are applications of principles to policy that the Catholic laity, with permission from their bishops, are free to accept or reject because they are judgments of prudence that may or may not be on target. The USCCB does not speak of social justice as a virtue to be practiced by the laity in all areas of life, but talks about it as a political condition brought about by the implementation of policy proposals. The bishops' conference, furthermore, doesn't offer guidance to the lay faithful on the practice of commutative justice, distributive justice, the cardinal virtue of justice, or St. Augustine's view of justice as the order in the soul, nor does it attempt to relate the various meanings of justice. The reason for these omissions seems to be the bishops' focus on promoting the adoption of good public policy as the primary way to practice social justice, rather than on educating the laity to understand and practice the different kinds of justice in all areas of their life.

A rather public example of the USCCB's approach to social justice can be seen in the reaction of an episcopal spokesperson to President Trump's decision on June 1, 2017, to withdraw the United States from the so-called Paris climate-change agreement. On the same day Bishop Oscar Cantu, chairman of the USCCB's Committee on International Justice and Peace, characterized the president's decision as "deeply troubling." Bishop Cantu went on to say, "The Scriptures affirm the value of caring for creation and caring for each other in solidarity. The Paris agreement is an international accord that promotes these values." He added, "President Trump's decision will harm the people of the United States and the world, especially the poorest, most vulnerable communities."[1] This kind of statement shuts down debate on the best way to address climate change and implies that faithful Catholics should adhere to the opinions of the political left on climate change. There is seemingly no openness to the possibility that there may be better ways to address climate change than that envisioned by the Paris accords. From my research I have found that the USCCB usually doesn't close off debate on an issue, but, as we just saw, frankly says that the Catholic laity may rightly take issue with episcopal policy proposals where there can be reasonable disagreement on the application of principles to policy.

By examining two of the many quadrennial statements the bishops issued during the year of a presidential election, I propose to reflect more deeply on the bishops' approach to social justice and some other aspects of the common good, and to suggest ways that they might deepen their influence on the political and social order. I have chosen statements issued in 2003 and 2007, respectively entitled *Faithful Citizenship: A Catholic Call to Political Responsibility* and *Forming Consciences for Faithful Citizenship: A Call to Political Responsibility from the Catholic Bishops of the United States*. A close look at these two statements indicate that the bishops drew more from the riches of Catholic social doctrine (CSD) in the 2007 statement, thereby attempting to overcome some of the limitations imposed by their longstanding approach to social justice, which is coming up with good public policy for the nation. A good example of the influence of CSD in the latter document is the emphasis on the education of the conscience of the lay faithful,

---

1   Catholic News Service (CNS), June 1, 2017.

an emphasis present in its very title. These documents are so different that comparing them is akin to describing a debate between two groups of bishops on the best way to promote social justice. It is likely that the arguments presented in the two statements will be used for quite some time by the differing groups of bishops, and therefore deserve a second look as history unfolds. Before delving into these two documents, let us briefly ponder what Catholic social doctrine says about the role of the bishops in the political order.

The Role of the Bishops in the Political Order

The ultimate end of the Church is the salvation of human beings, "which is to be achieved by faith in Christ and by his grace,"[2] and fully attained only in the afterlife.[3] Therefore, all the works of the Church have as their goal "the sanctification of men and women and the glorification of God in Christ."[4]

The specific mission that Christ entrusted to his Church, according to *Gaudium et spes*, "is not in the political, economic, or social order. The purpose which he set before her is a religious one."[5] Benedict XVI says, "The just ordering of society and the state is a central responsibility of politics." This work, always a political battle, is not the responsibility of the Church. What then is the role of the Church and its social doctrine with respect to justice? The aim of that doctrine "is simply to help purify reason and to contribute, here and now, to the acknowledgment and attainment of what is just." Because people are blinded by their interests and love of power, they have difficulty reasoning about justice and seeing what it requires in particular instances. To be an effective instrument, reason "must undergo constant purification." As a part of the work of purifying reason the Church forms the conscience of people, builds their character, and motivates them

2   Vatican Council II, *Apostolicam actuositatem* (*Decree on the Apostolate of the Laity*), no. 6.

3   Vatican Council II, *Gaudium et spes* (*Pastoral Constitution on the Church in the Modern World*), no. 40.

4   Vatican Council II, *Sacrosanctum concilium* (*Constitution on the Sacred Liturgy*), no. 10.

5   *Gaudium et spes*, no. 42.

to act justly. Still otherwise stated, the Church has a significant role in bringing about "openness of mind and will to the demands of the common good."[6] In this perspective the Church *indirectly*, but powerfully, contributes to the realization of justice in society and the state.

Although the Church's mission is salvation through sanctification, its mode of promoting justice has much to offer life in the city. Men and women receiving the message of salvation have the duty to imbue all temporal things with a Christian spirit. Out of the Church's religious mission, says *Gaudium et spes*, "comes a duty, a light, and an energy that can serve to structure and consolidate the human community according to divine law."[7] "The mission of the Church in its full range," Cardinal Dulles concludes, "may therefore be said to include not only the directly religious apostolate but also the penetration of the temporal sphere with the spirit of the Gospel (AA 5)."[8] As the Catholic Church has an obligation to foster peace and justice in the world, so popes and bishops rightfully and regularly address political, economic, and social matters, but not just like lay people.

At first glance it may seem that Vatican II is saying that the Church does and does not have a proper mission in the political, social, and economic order. Cardinal Dulles explains the apparent contradiction:

> To preach faith in Christ and to administer the sacraments are . . . proper to the Church. The Church was established precisely in order that these activities might be performed. But to erect a just and prosperous society is not . . . the proper business of the Church. To contribute to such a society is, however, a responsibility of Christians insofar as they are citizens of the earthly community. Unless they live up to their civic obligations they will be guilty in the sight of God. All Christians whether clergy or laity, have duties as members of the human community, but to

---

6   Benedict XVI, *Deus caritas est*, no. 28. The previous two quotations are also from no. 28 in *Deus caritas est*.

7   *Gaudium et spes*, no. 42.

8   Avery Dulles, *The Reshaping of Catholicism: Current Challenges in the Theology of the Church* (New York: Harper & Row, 1988), 147. Note that AA refers to Vatican II's *Decree on the Apostolate of the Laity*.

penetrate secular professions and organizations with the spirit of the gospel is preeminently the responsibility of the laity (GS 43; AA 7).[9]

In other words, the laity act as leaven in the world in every aspect of their lives.

Distinguishing the duties of clergy from those of the laity has been difficult since the end of Vatican Council II. Right at the beginning of his papacy John Paul II told bishops to pursue justice through evangelization,[10] to communicate Catholic social doctrine,[11] and to avoid anything that "resembles political party spirit or subjection to this or that ideology or system."[12] "Secular duties and activities belong properly although not exclusively to laymen."[13] These duties include the prudent application of Catholic social principles to public policy. In making such prudential judgments on the basis of shared goals, "it happens rather frequently, and legitimately, so," says Vatican II's *Gaudium et spes*, "that with equal sincerity some of the faithful will disagree with others on a given matter."[14] Where Catholics may legitimately disagree with one another is the domain of partisan politics.

The United States Conference of Catholic Bishops in the Political Order

Engagement in Partisan Politics

What about bishops engaging in partisan politics by taking positions on public policy? As mentioned, since the mid-1960s the U.S. bishops' conferences have been doing this on a regular basis. Is that the American way of communicating Catholic social doctrine, or does it resemble political party spirit? Surely, there are times when the principles of Catholic social

9   Dulles, *The Reshaping of Catholicism*, 148.
10   John Paul II, *John Paul II in Mexico* (London: Collins, 1979), 80.
11   *John Paul II in Mexico*, 82.
12   John Paul II, *Journey in the Light of the Eucharist* (Boston: Daughters of St. Paul, 1980), 349.
13   *Gaudium et spes*, no. 43.
14   *Gaudium et spes*, no. 43.

doctrine may overlap with partisan politics as commonly understood. There are times when the necessity of combating clear evils will require bishops to enter the policy arena. For example, Catholic doctrine requires opposition to unjust wars, the legalization of abortion, racism, etc. The question is whether ordinary partisan policy positions are appropriate for inclusion in episcopal pastoral letters or even in ordinary episcopal statements. In other words, should the bishops endorse one out of several legitimate approaches to tax, health care, welfare policy or climate control?

As I understand the arguments, the case for a social ministry focused on policy runs as follows. First, the U.S. Constitution gives all Americans, including bishops, the right to state their political opinions. Second, the simple proclamation of Catholic social principles is abstract and ineffective. No one will pay attention unless some policy is attacked or defended. Position-taking encourages people to reflect on the moral quality of their lives and moves them to action. Third, the root causes of injustice can be removed only by the right laws and structures. Furthermore, law shapes the mores of the nation. Where would we be without the Civil Rights Act of 1964? That Act certainly shows that policy removes evils. Fourth, Archbishop Rembert Weakland, chairman of the committee that wrote the economy pastoral of 1986, argued that the endorsement of specific, debatable policies in the letter is nothing new or extraordinary. He compared it on one occasion to the manner in which the Church specifies the duty to worship God by imposing a Sunday obligation. Archbishop Weakland's position is shared by many revisionist moral theologians. Still another argument is that a policy focus is simply the American way of being faithful to the exigencies of Vatican II and papal social teaching. Lastly, not seeking to benefit themselves, the bishops are not acting in a partisan manner.

In my judgment, these are not convincing arguments. The bishops should avoid a partisan policy focus in their pastoral letters, but not hesitate to be active participants in the public square when required by Catholic social doctrine or the presence of clear evils. Theological reasons support this position. First, the presence of nonbinding statements or mere political opinions in pastoral letters confuses the laity and further erodes episcopal authority. A Vatican official commented on the partisan nature of the second draft of the U.S. bishops' pastoral letter on war and peace:

> When bishops propose the doctrine of the church, the faithful
> are bound in conscience to assent. A serious problem arises on
> the pastoral level when bishops propose opinions based on the
> evaluation of technical or military factors. The faithful can be
> confused, their legitimate freedom of choice hindered, the
> teaching authority of bishops lessened and the influence of the
> church in society thus weakened.[15]

The faithful will be confused because most Catholics will have great difficulty distinguishing binding from nonbinding statements, especially since information will come largely from the secular media, which often do not grasp the essentials of Catholic teaching and may even deliberately slant reports to promote political programs.

Secondly, continuous teaching in the nonbinding mode leads to the opinion or even demand that the Church have a nonbinding category in the area of morals. This means that traditional Catholic teaching on moral matters, as expounded by the Magisterium, would be one opinion among many vying for acceptance. Cardinal Dulles also notes that the bishops must allow and even encourage dissent from their debatable political opinions. "The spirit of criticism and dissent thus unleashed can scarcely be prevented from spreading to strictly religious matters in which bishops have unquestionable authority in the church."[16] The laity, Cardinal Dulles implies, will have great difficulty drawing a line between proper and improper dissent from episcopal teaching. In other words, lay people may come to regard some authoritative Catholic teachings in the same light as ordinary political opinions.

Thirdly, the engagement of the Church in active partisan politics is not infrequently subsumed under the category of the prophetic mission of the Church. Calling nonbinding statements prophetic leads to a misunderstanding of Christianity itself. It is hard to imagine Amos or Isaiah saying to the Israelites, "These are my opinions with which you may legitimately disagree."

Fourthly, turning the episcopal conference into a lobby for good public policy necessarily diverts the attention of bishops from pressing internal

---

15   Jan Schotte, "A Vatican Synthesis," *Origins* 12 (1983), 693.
16   Dulles, *The Reshaping of Catholicism*, 178.

problems in the Church, such as the seminaries, catechesis, moral theology, and dissent from the Church's Magisterium. Many young people are growing up with little knowledge of Catholicism, no sense of the Church, and a narrow understanding of their obligations toward the common good. Reading about the policy proposals of the U.S. bishops will have little, if any, educational value for Catholics, especially because most of the information will come from the secular media. Because devising detailed policy proposals takes a lot of time and energy, Cardinal Dulles asks,

> Is it justified for [bishops] to go so far afield when many ecclesiastical matters, for which the bishops have inescapable responsibility, are crying out for greater attention? The impression is given that the bishops are more at ease in criticizing the performance of secular governments than in shouldering their own responsibilities in the Church.[17]

Cardinal Dulles also notes that the bishops could be sending the wrong message to lay people by their heavy involvement in politics. "When the bishops devote so much attention to worldly affairs they can unwittingly give the impression that what is truly important in their eyes is not the faith or holiness that leads to eternal life, but rather the structuring of human society to make the world more habitable."[18]

The response to the theological critique of the bishops' mode of political activity should not be a call for the Church to withdraw from the public arena. Rather, the hierarchical Church should be encouraged to have an even deeper impact on American culture and public policy, but to do so as Church—not as a typical lobby, not in such a way as to create false impressions. In criticizing certain kinds of partisan involvement on the part of bishops, I am hoping to foster greater episcopal influence on all matters of public concern. In other words, if the bishops speak about public problems as religious leaders and not as politicians or ordinary citizens, they will be more effective in promoting peace and justice.

---

17 *The Reshaping of Catholicism*, 176.
18 *The Reshaping of Catholicism*, 176.

Faithful Citizenship: A Catholic Call to Political Responsibility (2003)

Let us now turn to the two documents issued by the USCCB in 2003 and 2007 on "faithful citizenship." At first glance, many Catholics will regard the USCCB's *Faithful Citizenship* (2003) as a thoughtful, nonpartisan guide for voters. The bishops say they are exercising their responsibility to address the moral dimensions of public life and do so as pastors, not as partisan strategists. "A Catholic moral framework does not easily fit the ideologies of 'right' or 'left,' nor the platforms of any party. Our values are often not 'politically correct.'"[19] The bishops then call upon Catholics to be a community of conscience, to protect the dignity of the human person, and to promote the common good. In order to help Catholics do their civic duty the USCCB document poses ten questions for Catholics to consider as they make up their minds about the major issues facing the nation. Those questions are based on the bishops' formulation of seven themes in Catholic social teaching, namely: 1) the life and dignity of the human person; 2) the call to family, community, and participation; 3) rights and responsibilities; 4) the option for the poor and vulnerable; 5) the dignity of work and the rights of workers; 6) solidarity; and 7) caring for God's creation. Protecting the life and dignity of the human person is at the top of the list because it is the *sine qua non* of a sound and moral democracy.[20]

On the basis of the aforementioned seven themes of Catholic social teaching the USCCB comes up with four moral priorities for the public realm: protecting human life, promoting family life, pursuing social justice, and practicing global solidarity. Under the first rubric the bishops mention their strong opposition to abortion, euthanasia, cloning, the targeting of civilians by states or terrorists, the abuses of biotechnology, the preventive use of force, the death penalty, the failure of the U.S. both to sign the treaty banning the use of antipersonnel land mines and the Comprehensive Test Ban Treaty, and the U.S. participation in "the scandalous global trade in arms."[21]

---

19 United States Conference of Catholic Bishops Administrative Committee, *Faithful Citizenship*, 7.

20 *Faithful Citizenship*, 4–6.

21 *Faithful Citizenship*, 17–19.

To promote family life the bishops endorse the legal protection of marriage "as a lifelong commitment between a man and a woman."[22] The bishops also call for just wages to those who support families, the protection and education of children including the formation of their character in educational settings, the safeguarding of the parental right to choose private or public education for their children, and the enforcement of responsible regulations to protect children from pornography and violent material on television, the radio, and the Internet.[23]

The third and fourth priorities are social justice[24] and global solidarity.[25] Under the rubric of social justice the USCCB Committee recommends the following: "jobs for all who can work," a living wage, the end of unjust discrimination at work, the right of all workers to organize, "economic freedom, initiative, and the right to private property," welfare reform that doesn't cut programs and resources, and "tax credits, health care, child care, and safe, affordable housing." The Committee further supports the work of faith-based groups as a partner with government, income security during retirement for the "low- and average-wage workers and their families," "affordable and accessible health care for all," the strengthening of Medicare and Medicaid, government aid for those suffering from HIV/AIDS and various addictions, affordable housing for all through contributions from the public and private sector, "food security for all," sufficient income for farmers, better treatment of farm workers, policies that "support sustainable agriculture" and respect the earth, better treatment of immigrants, quality education for all, more just salaries for teachers and administrators, and the provision of the typical public school services in private and religious schools. The bishops then call on the nation to address the culture of violence, especially in the media; they recommend tighter gun control measures, the end to the death penalty, and the continuation of the battle against discrimination, with the help of affirmative action programs. Finally, they urge "care for the earth and for the environment," attention to global climate change, energy conservation, and the development of new, clean energy sources.

---

22 *Faithful Citizenship*, 20.
23 *Faithful Citizenship*, 20–21.
24 *Faithful Citizenship*, 22–26.
25 *Faithful Citizenship*, 26–28

Under the fourth priority, "practicing global solidarity," the USCCB urges the United States to take "a leading role in helping to *alleviate global poverty*," to make more efforts to promote *religious* liberty and other human rights around the world, "to reverse the spread of *nuclear, chemical, and biological weapons*, and to reduce its own reliance on weapons of mass destruction by pursing progressive nuclear disarmament." The bishops further recommend more political and financial support for "appropriate United Nations programs, other international bodies, and international law," and they call upon the United States to adopt a more generous immigration policy, especially for those fleeing persecution. Finally, they urge the government to be a leader, "in collaboration with the international community, in addressing *regional conflicts* in the Middle East, the Balkans, the Congo, Sudan, Colombia, and West Africa." The USCCB places special emphasis on the U.S. role in helping to resolve the Israeli-Palestinian conflict with security for Israel, a state for the Palestinians, and peace for all. The bishops also urge the government, together with members of the international community, to persevere in working "to help bring stability, democracy, freedom and prosperity to *Iraq and Afghanistan*."[26]

Although the USCCB doesn't list all its legislative priorities or give much detail about the issues it discusses, readers can still form a pretty good idea of where the bishops stand on the political spectrum. In terms of the sheer number of items the USCCB's agenda is more Democratic than Republican. But, in terms of their first two priorities, protecting human life and promoting family life, the USCCB's agenda favors Republicans over Democrats, unless Catholics think that opposition to the Bush Administration's Iraq policy and its war on terrorism must take precedence over opposition to abortion and euthanasia. (The death penalty is supported by a majority of both Republicans and Democrats.) What conclusions does the bishops' Administrative Committee want Catholics to draw from reading their pre-election document?

The bishops offer their readers an overarching principle to guide them in the evaluation of all the issues, namely, the "consistent ethic of life."

26 *Faithful Citizenship*, 29.

We do not wish to instruct persons on how they should vote by endorsing or opposing candidates. We hope that voters will examine the position of candidates on the full range of issues, as well as on their personal integrity, philosophy and performance. We are convinced that a consistent ethic of life should be the moral framework from which to address issues in the political arena.[27]

On the contrary, the USCCB does implicitly instruct voters, not by endorsing or opposing candidates, but by laying out its own policy positions and by suggesting that Catholics evaluate candidates for office in light of those positions, within the moral framework provided by "the consistent ethic of life," keeping in mind the character, the political vision, and past performance of the candidates.

What does this "consistent ethic of life" entail? Generally, it is a term used in social justice circles to describe the position that those who object to the taking of life at one stage or in one form must object to the taking of life at all stages and in all forms. Practically speaking, this means that those who oppose abortion should in practice oppose capital punishment and most wars. It is also generally understood to mean that Catholics should promote a respect-life attitude by supporting government spending on what are called the "social justice" issues, and embrace a host of progressive priorities. This is a position articulated by the late Cardinal Joseph Bernardin, the former Archbishop of Chicago, who argued in his much discussed Fordham address of December 6, 1983, that a consistent ethic of life not only opposes abortion but also endorses policies designed to increase a people's well-being, that is, their quality of life. Cardinal Bernardin argued, "A quality of life posture translates into specific political and economic positions on tax policy, employment generation, welfare policy, nutrition and feeding programs and health care."[28]

Anyone who is consistently pro-life and on the side of justice should favor the kind of governmental policy that will help everyone, especially

---

27 *Faithful Citizenship*, 11.
28 Cardinal Joseph Bernardin, "Call for a Consistent Ethic of Life," *Origins* 13, no. 29 (1983), 493.

the poor. Reasonable Catholics, nevertheless, might disagree as to which policies will do the most good. So, Cardinal Bernardin interprets "the consistent ethic of life" to mean both opposition to clear evils about which there should be no dispute, and the endorsement of specific positions on such matters as tax policy, about which there will inevitably and legitimately be disagreement. *Faithful Citizenship* implicitly reflects the same interpretation of "the consistent ethic of life."

The bishops attempt to clarify what the "consistent ethic" requirement means by quoting from the Vatican *Doctrinal Note on Some Questions Regarding the Participation of Catholics in Political Life*.

> A well-formed Christian conscience does not permit one to vote for a political program or an individual law which contradicts the fundamental contents of faith and morals. The Christian faith is an integral unity, and thus it is incoherent to isolate some particular element to the detriment of the whole of Catholic doctrine. A political commitment to a single isolated aspect of the Church's social doctrine does not exhaust one's responsibility towards the common good.[29]

Unfortunately, the bishops do not offer an explanation of this quotation. They simply urge Catholics to adhere to moral principles, practice discernment, and make "prudential judgments based on the values of our faith."[30] Then they mention the seven moral principles or themes of Catholic social teaching and explain their four moral priorities for public life.

The bishops comment on such a dizzying array of political issues that their readers will be hard-pressed to distinguish which ones should have priority for Catholics, especially when *Faithful Citizenship* argues that "some Catholics may feel politically homeless, sensing that no political party and too few candidates share a consistent concern for human life and dignity."[31]

---

29 *Faithful Citizenship*, 12, quoting Congregation for the Doctrine of the Faith, *Doctrinal Note on Some Questions Regarding the Participation of Catholics in Political Life* (November 24, 2002), no. 4.

30 *Faithful Citizenship*, 12.

31 *Faithful Citizenship*, 3.

The bishops' Administrative Committee is apparently not heartened—even though pro-choice supporters are dismayed—by George Bush's position on abortion. In other words, both the Republicans and Democrats fail to measure up to the high standards of Catholic social teaching. The message seems to be that each party is more or less equally deficient.

When all is said and done, *Faithful Citizenship* may be interpreted by Catholics as a permission to vote for a pro-abortion candidate if his position on other issues supports enough items on the USCCB's political agenda. The Catholic faithful will receive an additional incentive to think this way from pro-abortion Democrats who can display high marks on their "Catholic voting scorecard." Did the bishops intend this state of affairs, one may ask? Surely not. Nevertheless, previous USCCB documents on faithful citizenship and political responsibility have been so interpreted by people with an interest in voting for liberal candidates, despite their pro-choice stance.

Many Catholics may interpret the "consistent ethic of life" to mean that a candidate who is against abortion, euthanasia, the destruction of embryos in research, cloning, same-sex marriage, etc., does not deserve their vote if he or she supported the recent war in Iraq, believes in the death penalty, and doesn't support certain poverty programs. Put another way, Catholics might read the document to mean that a candidate who is adamantly "pro-choice" and a supporter of same-sex marriage might be worthy of their vote if he also favors generous antipoverty legislation, minority rights, job training for the poor and underprivileged, increased educational opportunities for the poor, and opposition to war and the death penalty. This is a likely scenario because the USCCB doesn't explicitly argue that some evils are more serious than others and, therefore, should be addressed above all. While listing abortion and euthanasia as the first moral priorities for public life might incline some readers to take these evils more seriously than others, *Faithful Citizenship* avoids the dramatic language used both by John Paul II in his *Gospel of Life* about the culture of death, and by the USCCB itself in statements specifically addressing the evil of abortion. Not noticing any special urgency, Catholics might also conclude that abortion is not that much of a priority if the pro-life candidate is judged to be the cause of x number of other evils, or insufficiently committed to the USCCB's positions on social justice and global solidarity.

My point will perhaps become clearer by taking a brief look at Michael Pakaluk's critique of Cardinal Bernardin's "seamless garment" or "consistent ethic theory." Pakaluk says it would make no sense to argue that the South before 1865 was unjust because of the institution of slavery and because the roads were not properly maintained in poorer regions. While the latter would be a problem, it would simply pale in relation to the evil of slavery. To think about the relation of abortion to other evils Pakaluk suggests that there are two ways of conceiving the evils of abortion.

> The first is that abortion is a calamity, a moral catastrophe of the first order, like the Ukrainian famine or the Holocaust. On this view, legalized abortion constitutes a direct attack on the foundation of our society: it involves the destruction of the most fundamental human bonds and requires, perilously, the continued corruption of our legal and medical professions. Our immediate task as citizens is to work with an almost militant commitment . . . to remove this evil.[32]

According to this view, the primary duty of all citizens, especially Catholics, is do everything morally possible to oppose the evil of abortion.

The second way of looking at abortion, argues Pakaluk, is to look at it as one of many evils threatening the polity. "These evils come and go over time; and . . . we simply have to do our best to bring about the best society that we can achieve."[33] According to this way of looking at things, faithful citizens may vote for pro-abortion candidates who seem to oppose more evils than pro-life candidates. "The seamless garment theory," argues Pakaluk, "gives no support to the first view, which follows logically from the very nature of abortion conceded by Bernardin, and encourages the second view, which is a formula for lukewarmness and apathy."[34]

Unfortunately, *Faithful Citizenship* doesn't present abortion as a calamity of the first order, as the bishops do in some of their fine statements on

32 Michael Pakaluk, "A Cardinal Error: Does the Seamless Garment Make Sense?", *Crisis* 6, no. 10 (1988), 14.
33 Pakaluk, *Crisis* 6, no. 10 (1988), 14.
34 Pakaluk, *Crisis* 6, no. 10 (1988), 14.

human life. The document's focus on the "consistent ethic of life" reflects more Cardinal Bernardin's seamless garment theory than it does John Paul II's *Gospel of Life*.

Besides the problems posed by the USCCB's "consistent ethic of life" theory, *Faithful Citizenship*, unfortunately, has the potential of misleading Catholics in a number of other areas. In comparing the Vatican's *Doctrinal Note* with the bishops' statement, one immediately notices that the former understands better than the latter the distinction between Church teaching and partisan politics, the importance of bishops being pastors and not partisan strategists, the indispensability of the practice of virtue for the reform of the political order, the devastating effect of relativism on society and the political order, the hierarchy of evils in society, how imperative it is for the Church to oppose the legalization of same-sex marriage, and the necessity of giving directives to Catholic politicians. A comparison of papal social teaching and other USCCB statements with *Faithful Citizenship* reveals that the latter omits to mention the many ways citizens may help the poor and promote social justice besides having the right opinion on the issues and voting for the best candidates.

Let us first look at the understanding of partisanship in *Faithful Citizenship*. The bishops realize that their own policy proposals may not always be the best way to realize their goals. That's why, as mentioned, they openly state in various places that lay Catholics may reasonably disagree with their approach. They actually admit their partisanship in both their pastoral letters on war and peace (1983) and on the economy (1986). In the former they write, "At times we state universally binding moral principles found in the teaching of the Church; at other times the pastoral letter makes specific applications, observations and recommendations which allow for diversity of opinion on the part of those who assess the factual data of a situation differently."[35] In the latter they alert their readers to their partisanship by writing, "We know that some of our specific recommendations are controversial. As bishops, we do not claim to make these prudential judgments with the same kind of authority that marks our declarations of

---

35 National Conference of Catholic Bishops, *The Challenge of Peace: God's Promise and Our Response: A Pastoral Letter on War and Peace* (Washington, D.C.: United States Catholic Conference, 1983), I.

principle."[36] Given this admission, I am constantly baffled when they affirm that their conference is not partisan. In *Faithful Citizenship* the bishops say, "As an institution, we are called to be *political but not partisan*. The Church cannot be a chaplain for any one party or cheerleader for any candidate."[37] The bishops seem to think that they can avoid the charge of partisanship as long as they don't endorse a candidate or a party. In fact, any time they endorse policy positions with which reasonable Catholics may disagree they are acting in a partisan manner. They are rightly political when they teach the whole faith, explain all of Catholic social teaching, call for the end of clear evils, and inspire an educated and virtuous laity to change the world.

Cardinal Avery Dulles, before he became a cardinal, directed attention to the bizarre claim made by the bishops that they are speaking as pastors when they

> enter into technical realms such as counterforce targeting of military objectives . . . the minimum wage law, progressive taxation and affirmative action. The bishops claim to be speaking as pastors, not as experts on military affairs, economics or whatever. But when they make detailed applications of the kind I have mentioned, this distinction is hard to maintain.[38]

Let us recall the teaching of the Vatican's *Doctrinal Note*. Since there are various political opinions compatible with faith and the moral law, "it is not the Church's task, to set forth specific political solutions—and even less to propose a single solution as the acceptable one—to temporal questions that God has left to the free and responsible judgment of each single person."[39] There is a good reason behind this position. If bishops endorse debatable policy solutions to specific problems, "they stir up opposition to themselves within the church," says Cardinal Avery Dulles, "and undermine

---

36 National Conference of Catholic Bishops, *Economic Justice For All: Pastoral Letter on Catholic Social Teaching and the U.S. Economy* (Washington, D.C.: United States Catholic Conference, Inc.), xii.

37 *Faithful Citizenship*, 29.

38 Avery Dulles, "Religion and the Transformation of Politics," *America* 167, no 12 (1992), 297.

39 Congregation for the Doctrine of the Faith, *Doctrinal Note*, no. 3.

their own authority to teach and govern." Since the end of Vatican Council II, the bishops' conferences have continuously entered the world of partisan politics by making choices among policy proposals "that are held by sincere and intelligent Catholics."[40] It is true that the number of bishops appreciating the wisdom of Dulles' point does seem to be growing. As we will soon see, at least some of these bishops did have an influence on the content of the next document that was issued in the fall of 2007 to guide Catholics in the 2008 election.

Even though the bishops are obviously people of good will trying their best to benefit society, the USCCB's denial of partisanship is not a harmless mistake. If Catholics are convinced that bishops are never partisan, they may elevate the bishops' debatable policy proposals to the level of doctrine. Such a move will further skew the interpretation of "the consistent ethic of life." If a pro-choice candidate supports twenty-five of the USCCB's policy proposals on social justice and global solidarity, won't many Catholics be induced to downplay his support of abortion in the light of his "non-partisan," Catholic positions on social justice?

Another problem with the USCCB's *Faithful Citizenship* is the failure to tell Catholics that faithful citizenship includes much more than voting for good public policy. *Faithful Citizenship* claims to be "a statement on the responsibilities of Catholics to society." In fact, it doesn't really address this large topic at all. It is simply a guide to the issues facing the nation in the election of 2004. If the USCCB had just spelled out the implications of the spiritual and corporal works of mercy, it would, indeed, have been a good beginning for a statement on how Catholics could contribute to the well-being of society. In no place does the USCCB call upon the laity to make a contribution to civil society, except through some kind of political action. The episcopal conference chooses not to point out their own belief, professed elsewhere, that civil society offers Catholics an opportunity to be good citizens at work, in their families and neighborhoods, and in their volunteer activities. Failure to make this point unwittingly gives Catholics the idea that they can be good citizens simply by supporting good public policy through their votes.

A document that really focused on the responsibilities of Catholics toward society would have approached their four priority issues in a more

40 Dulles, "Religion and the Transformation of Politics," 297.

comprehensive way. For example, in the section on promoting family life, where the bishops call for the legal protection of traditional marriage, they could also have called upon Catholic clergy and laity to persevere in their efforts to prepare the young for marriage by educating them in the faith and by persuading them to practice chastity before and after marriage. Ignorance of the faith, premarital promiscuity and cohabitation as well as the practice of contraception in marriage are obstacles to living out the Church teaching on the sacrament of matrimony. Here was a perfect opportunity to point out that the separation of sex from its essential connection to procreation through the practice of contraception has prepared the way for acceptance of same-sex marriage. The section on social justice could have made the point that two of the most effective, long-term solutions to the problem of poverty are intact families and the work of Catholic education in poor neighborhoods. There are Catholic schools throughout the country that have done a wonderful job educating the poor, both Catholic and non-Catholic. They could even do better with more resources.

A fourth, and most serious, omission in *Faithful Citizenship* is the failure to address Catholic politicians on the subject of abortion and same-sex marriage. Surprisingly, the USCCB doesn't take Catholic legislators to task for their persistent support of the right to abortion and for resorting to the subterfuge that they are personally opposed to abortion but wouldn't think of trying to persuade others to share their opinion. This is like a pre-Civil War politician saying, "I am personally opposed to slavery, but won't support a law banning slavery." At least, they could have spoken like Archbishop Charles Chaput of Denver, who said,

> We've come a long way from John F. Kennedy, who merely locked his faith in the closet. Now we have Catholic senators who take pride in arguing for legislation that threatens and destroys life—and who then also take Communion. The kindest explanation for this sort of behavior is that a lot of Catholic candidates don't know their own faith.[41]

41 Archbishop Charles Chaput, "How to Tell a Duck from a Fox: Thinking with the Church as We Look toward November," *Denver Catholic Register*, April 14, 2004. This article is available on the website of the Archdiocese of Denver.

Furthermore, the bishops neither call upon the Catholic politicians to oppose the legalization of "marriage" between persons of the same sex nor alert Catholics in their document to the movement in the country to legalize same-sex marriage. This omission reveals a lack of political prudence, given the real possibility that the legalization of same-sex marriage will change the public understanding of marriage entirely. This is in stark contrast to the Vatican effort to provide specific guidelines to Catholic politicians in a statement issued on June 3, 2003, entitled *Regarding Proposals To Give Legal Recognition To Unions Between Homosexual Persons*. Catholic politicians are instructed to oppose any laws which give legal recognition to same-sex unions. If laws are passed giving such legal recognition, Catholic politicians must make their opposition known and work to have the laws repealed. The Congregation for the Doctrine of the Faith states its rationale for its position as follows:

> Society owes its continued survival to the family, founded on marriage. The inevitable consequence of legal recognition of homosexual unions would be the redefinition of marriage which would become, in its legal status, an institution devoid of essential reference to factors linked to heterosexuality; for example, procreation and raising children.[42]

While the USCCB missed an opportunity in *Faithful Citizenship* to contribute more to the political education of Catholics, especially Catholic politicians, the bishops addressed this lacuna in their meeting of June 2004. After the June meeting the USCCB issued "Catholics in Political Life," a two-page statement prepared by its Task Force on Catholic Bishops and Catholic Politicians with the collaboration of two additional bishops and a cardinal, and then modified by the entire body of bishops during their meeting. This short statement, developed on the basis of their more extensive interim report, is obviously not the final word.

"Catholics in Political Life" makes the following points. 1) "If those who perform an abortion and those who cooperate willingly in the action are fully

---

42   Congregation for the Doctrine of the Faith, *Regarding Proposals to Give Legal Recognition to Unions Between Homosexual Persons*, III, no. 8.

aware of objective evil of what they do, they are guilty of grave sin and thereby separate themselves from God's grace." 2) "Those who formulate law . . . have an obligation in conscience to work toward correcting morally defective laws, lest they be guilty of cooperating in evil and in sinning against the common good." The bishops mention the legalization of abortion on demand as an example of a morally defective law. 3) The bishops "counsel Catholic public officials that their acting consistently to support abortion on demand risks making them cooperators in evil in a public manner." Note that they don't say that pro-choice Catholic politicians are definitely cooperating in evil or are in an objective state of sin. The bishops seem to imply that Catholic pro-choice politicians may not know that supporting the legalization of abortion is formal cooperation in evil. They then express the hope that the proper formation of their consciences will deter Catholic politicians from supporting the right to abortion. 4) All Catholics have an obligation to defend human life and human dignity in public life. 5) Catholic institutions should not honor Catholics who act against the fundamental moral teachings of the Catholic Church. 6) It is up to individual bishops to decide whether to deny communion to pro-choice Catholic politicians. (Of the seventy bishops who submitted an opinion to the Task Force, those opposing the denial of Holy communion to pro-choice Catholic politicians prevailed by a margin of three to one. 7) The bishops commit themselves to "to continue to *teach* clearly and help other Catholic leaders to teach clearly on our unequivocal commitment to the legal protection of human life from the moment of conception until natural death." 8) The bishops further recognize that they "need to do more to *persuade* all people that human life is precious and human dignity must be defended." To accomplish this goal the USCCB says that "more effective dialogue and engagement" with Catholic politicians is necessary. 9) "All must examine their conscience as to their worthiness to receive the Body and Blood of our Lord. This examination includes fidelity to the moral teaching of the Church in personal and public life."

These points in "Catholics in Political Life" fill a big gap in *Faithful Citizenship*, which had nothing to say about or to pro-choice Catholic politicians. The strong point of this statement is their commitment to persuade pro-choice Catholic politicians to recognize they are not in communion with the Church and to refrain from receiving the Eucharist out of a sense of integrity. One should not underestimate how important this point is.

Forming Consciences for Faithful Citizenship: A Call to Political Responsibility from the Catholic Bishops of the United States (2007)

Let us now turn to the 2007 quadrennial statement on the political responsibility of Catholics, which was issued under the signature of the entire body of bishops. The General Secretary noted at the very end of the text, however, that it "was developed by the chairmen, in consultation with the membership, of the Committees on Domestic Policy, International Policy, Pro-Life Activities, Communications, Doctrine, Education, and Migration of the United States Catholic Conference of Bishops (USCCB)." Despite being a document of many committees, it is a vast improvement over its immediate predecessor, thanks in some measure to the work of the USCCB's Committee on Doctrine in coordinating the input from all the participating committees and from individual bishops throughout the country. The Committee on Pro-Life Activities obviously had much more influence on the 2007 document than on the one issued in 2003, when the Committee on Domestic and International Policy wielded the most influence. It is still something of a compromise document because the USCCB's committees are representative of the split between liberal and conservative Catholics on questions of justice and the common good. I will not summarize the whole document but will direct attention to its new tone, organization, and clearly stated priorities, and then I will suggest that a fuller explanation of some themes drawn from Catholic social doctrine should be included.

There are three parts to *Forming Consciences for Faithful Citizenship: A Call to Political Responsibility from the Catholic Bishops of the United States*. Part I (no. 1–62), the most important part of the document, speaks of forming the consciences of Catholics for political life and presents, through an explanation of seven themes, what the Catholic Church has to say about the role Catholic social teaching should play in the public square. The seven themes are exactly the same ones discussed in the 2003 statement. Part II (no. 63–88) applies the principles of Catholic social teaching to the issues arising in the areas of human life, family life, social justice, and global solidarity, also in the same way as the bishops did in 2003. The emphasis on forming consciences, however, is a completely new tack, especially in that it exhorts lay people to acquire the virtue of prudence. Part III (no. 89–

90) lists ten goals for political life in a way meant to challenge citizens, candidates, and public officials. This is a completely new tack as well. What's new in this quadrennial document goes a long way to remedy the deficiencies I have noted in the previous one.

In the very beginning of the introduction to Part I the bishops draw attention to the fact that "the right to life itself is not fully protected, especially for unborn children, the most vulnerable members of the American family" (no. 2). Right away the reader realizes that abortion is going to be a priority. Shortly afterwards, they cite a very important statement from Vatican Council II's *Declaration on Religious Liberty* (no. 6) on the relation between the practice of the faith and the attainment of justice. The declaration says, "Society itself may enjoy the benefits of justice and peace, which result from [people's] faithfulness to God and his holy will." The bishops comment, "The work for justice requires that the mind and the heart of Catholics be educated and formed to know and practice the whole faith" (no. 4). This point may seem very obvious, but is hardly, if ever, mentioned by influential Catholics. Yet the whole endeavor of Catholic social doctrine depends on the widespread practice of the entire Catholic faith—as already mentioned.

Toward the end of the introduction the bishops say that their purpose in writing "is to help Catholics form their consciences in accordance with God's truth" (no. 7). With a properly formed conscience, one oriented toward social charity, the lay faithful can more effectively participate in political life by voting and other means. Noteworthy is the bishops' point that voting does not by any means exhaust one's political responsibility. The service of the common good requires many different initiatives. Quoting the *Catechism of the Catholic Church*, the bishops say that "it is necessary that all participate, each according to his position and role, in promoting the common good. This obligation is inherent in the dignity of the human person. . . . As far as possible citizens should take an active part in *public life*" (no. 1913–1915). The implication of this statement is that fulfilling duties is a way of being faithful to one's dignity. In other words, not carrying out duties in life is to act beneath one's dignity. So, dignity is not just an inalienable given but a quality that is achieved by the way one lives. This is an observation that the USCCB does not make when it directly explains the meaning of human dignity.

The bishops also clearly distinguish their role in the public square from that of the laity. Quoting Benedict XVI, the bishops explain that the "Church cannot take upon itself the political battle to bring about the most just society possible" (*Deus caritas est*, no. 28); "the direct duty to work for a just ordering of society is proper to the lay faithful" (*Deus caritas est*, no. 29). The role of the Church is to form consciences by teaching Catholic social doctrine. The laity, then, enter into the political fray and work for the implementation of policies and laws that will promote justice.

The bishops next elaborate on the meaning of conscience and form the consciences of the lay faithful by exhorting them to acquire the virtue of prudence. A prudent person recognizes that there are some things that neither individuals nor society can do because they are *intrinsically evil*. "A prime example is the intentional taking of innocent human life, as in abortion and euthanasia" (no. 22). Other examples include genocide, racism, torture, "and the targeting of non-combatants in acts of terror or war" (no. 23). A prudent person also realizes that people must do good in the public square by choosing policies that will improve the economy, food distribution, health care, the chances of peace in Iraq, etc. "The moral imperative to respond to the needs of our neighbors . . . is universally binding on our consciences and may be legitimately fulfilled by a variety of means" (no. 25). In other words, faithful Catholics may legitimately disagree on which policies will improve the economy or promote better health care. This has to be the case since there are so many factors to be considered and such difficulty in grasping all the particulars that pertain to a good economy and good health care. Just because the work is difficult doesn't excuse people from helping those in need. As Thomas Aquinas noted, people will have various levels of abilities in discerning the positive initiatives that should be taken to promote the common good in the public square; all good people, however, should be able to recognize intrinsically evil actions.

To make sure they are not misunderstood the bishops mention again that rejecting intrinsically evil actions and embracing a particular solution to the healthcare problem are very different moral actions. "The direct and intentional destruction of innocent human life from the moment of conception until natural death is always wrong and is not just one issue among many. It must always be opposed" (no. 28). The bishops quote John Paul II to reinforce their point: "'Above all, the common outcry, which is justly made on behalf of human rights—for example, the right to health, to home, to work, to family, to culture—is false and illusory if *the right to life,* the most basic and fundamental right and the condition for all other personal rights, is not defended with maximum determination.' (*Christifideles laici,* no. 38)." In other words, the virtue of prudence doesn't allow a faithful Catholic to say that a particular political candidate's policy proposals with respect to the economy, health care, and energy are so good that his acceptance of abortion and euthanasia, intrinsically evil actions, doesn't matter all that much. Respecting the right to life always remains a priority, even for the attainment of social and political rights. In addition, "A Catholic cannot vote for a candidate who takes a position in favor of an intrinsic evil action, such as abortion or racism, if the voter's intent is to support that position" (no. 34). Catholics may never approve of intrinsically evil actions for any reason whatsoever. There can be no exception to this principle.

The next question that naturally arises is this one: "Can Catholics vote for pro-abortion candidates, not because of their anti-life stance, but in spite of it, because they are right on so many other matters?" The bishops respond very carefully. "There may be times when a Catholic who rejects a candidate's unacceptable position may decide to vote for that candidate for other morally grave reasons. Voting in this way would be permissible for truly grave moral reasons, not to advance narrow interests or partisan preferences or to ignore a fundamental evil act" (no. 35). Unfortunately, the bishops do not elaborate on the meaning of *"grave moral reasons,"* but their previous remarks imply that Cardinal Justin Rigali was right to say in an interview with the *National Catholic Register,* "That is the core of the document—that the 'obligation to oppose intrinsically evil acts has a special claim on our consciences and actions.'" (Cardinal Rigali is actually quoting from no. 37 in the document.) The very designation of various actions as "intrinsically evil" marks them as calamities in the moral order. By speaking in this way the bishops have made crystal clear that opposition to abortion and opposition to a particular economic or energy policy are of an entirely different order. While Catholics are not single-issue voters, "a candidate's position on a single issue that involves an intrinsic evil, such as support for legal abortion or the promotion of racism, may legitimately lead a voter to disqualify a candidate from receiving support" (no. 42). Reasonable Catholics may legitimately disagree about economic and energy policy, but not on what is intrinsically evil. To vote for a candidate who supports intrinsically evil acts, the bishops imply, requires very compelling reasons, a standard not easily met. Nevertheless, we all know that Catholics will interpret "grave moral reasons" in a variety of unpersuasive ways, even if the bishops were more explicit about their understanding of the term. In other words, many Catholics will vote for pro-choice candidates if they are perceived to have good policy suggestions, say, on global warming, energy policy, and the housing crisis.

In a short document the bishops could not elaborate much on the seven themes of Catholic social doctrine that they mention. Nevertheless, they would do the laity a great service by clarifying the meaning of human dignity. The dignity of the human person is both a given and a goal, laboriously achieved over a lifetime. If Christians can act beneath their dignity by sinning, they can also live in accordance with it by practicing virtue in every aspect of their lives. In discussing the theme of family, the bishops specifically mention the harm of "permitting same-sex unions or other distortions of marriage" (no. 46). *Faithful Citizenship* of 2003 omitted this point in its discussion of the family.

The section on rights and responsibilities improves the 2003 document by laying stress on the importance of religious freedom and freedom of conscience. Following the lead of John Paul II and Benedict XVI, they say, "In a fundamental way, the right to free expression of religious beliefs protects all other rights" (no. 49). Given the various attempts on the part of governments around the world to restrict religious freedom, this is a very important addition.

The discussion on caring for God's creation is also an improvement on the 2003 treatment because it issues a particular challenge to individuals: "We should strive to live simply to meet the needs of the present without compromising the ability of future generations to meet their own needs" (no. 54).

In the conclusion the bishops draw attention to the limits of politics and to the importance of implementing the principle of subsidiarity. In its work to achieve the common good the state is aided by the actors in civil society. "Building a world of respect for human life and dignity, where justice and peace prevail, requires more than just political commitment. Individuals, families, businesses, community organizations, and governments all have a role to play" (no. 57).

Part II explains how the bishops themselves apply Catholic social teaching to the major issues of the day under the rubrics of human life, family life, social justice, and global solidarity. There is not much difference between the 2003 and 2007 documents in this section, with a few exceptions. The bishops begin by explaining that some of their observations must be accepted by all Catholics because they involve fundamental moral principles; with respect to the application of some principles to the issues, the bishops acknowledge that others may legitimately apply the principles in a different way. "While people of good will may sometimes choose different ways to apply and act on some of our principles, Catholics cannot ignore their inescapable moral challenges or simply dismiss the Church's guidance or policy directions that flow from these principles" (no. 63). Earlier in the document they had said, "The judgments and recommendations that we make as bishops on specific issues do not carry the same moral authority as statements of universal moral teaching" (no. 33). These are important caveats because lay Catholics may legitimately apply principles to many issues on the basis of their own well-formed consciences in ways that differ from positions taken by the USCCB. Despite the bishops' admission of diminished authority, I still think they are making a mistake teaching in this nonbinding mode for reasons already explained earlier in this chapter.

In the section on family life the bishops add a comment about coercive contraception programs and freedom of conscience. "We oppose contraceptive mandates in public programs and health plans, which endanger rights of conscience and can interfere with parents' rights to guide the moral formation of their children" (no. 71). The section on social justice contains an additional paragraph indicating that "the religious duty of stewardship" requires care of the earth (no. 87). In the section on global solidarity the bishops urge the United States not to support programs imposing contraception on the poor people of the world. "Our nation's efforts to reduce poverty should not be associated with demeaning and sometimes coercive population control programs; instead these efforts should focus on working with the poor to help them build a future of hope and opportunity for themselves and their children" (no. 88). This is an important addendum given what is happening at international conferences throughout the world. Many actors in the international arena are seeking to impose contraception on the poor.

In the new third and final section of their 2007 document, the bishops list their ten goals for political life. The first three goals reflect the bishops' priorities revealed earlier in the document: 1) end the legalization of abortion; 2) avoid using violence to address fundamental problems: "a million abortions each year to deal with unwanted pregnancies, euthanasia and assisted suicide to deal with the burdens of illness and disability, the destruction of human embryos in the name of research, the use of the death penalty to combat crime, and imprudent resort to war to address international disputes" (no. 90); and 3) "Define the central institution of marriage as a union between one man and one woman, and provide better support for family life morally, socially, and economically so that our nation helps parents raise their children with respect for life, sound moral values, and an ethic of stewardship and responsibility" (no. 90). The other seven goals deal with such things as immigration, poverty, health care, discrimination, encouragement of all to pursue the common good, the use of military force, and human rights.

This 2007 statement is an immense improvement over its 2003 predecessor, which will, unfortunately, remain a beguiling alternative in the years to come for not a few Catholics. One thing is certain: on the campuses of Catholic universities the faculty with an orientation toward social justice are more likely to invoke the 2003 statement because of its reliance on the so-called consistent ethic of life. Many Catholics interpret this theory to mean that they can vote for the liberal agenda with a clear conscience, even though it includes support for same-sex marriage and the untrammeled right to choose abortion and other anti-life measures.[43]

The importance of the emphasis on the formation of the conscience of the lay faithful cannot be overestimated. Successful formation of conscience over a long period of time will put many of the lay faithful in a position to be a leaven in all areas of social life. The bishops cannot transform the political and social order by themselves. They need the cooperation of a well-informed, faith-filled, and dedicated laity.

---

43   For a more complete treatment of the Church's contribution to the political order, especially the role of Catholic laity, see J. Brian Benestad, *Church, State, and Society: An Introduction to Catholic Social Doctrine* (Washington, D.C.: Catholic University of America Press, 2011), 215–53. Material in this chapter was drawn from that book.

Contributors

J. Brian Benestad (Ph.D., Boston College) is the D'Amour Chair of Catholic Thought at Assumption College and the author of *Church, State, and Society: An Introduction to Catholic Social Doctrine* (Catholic University of America Press, 2011).

Jean Bethke Elshtain (1941–2013) was the Laura Spelman Rockefeller Professor of Social and Political Ethics at the University of Chicago Divinity School and author of *Sovereignty: God, State, Self* (Gifford Lectures, 2008).

John Finnis is Professor Emeritus of Law & Legal Philosophy at Oxford University and Biolchini Family Professor of Law at the University of Notre Dame Law School. He is the author of *Natural Law and Natural Rights* (Oxford University Press, 2d ed. 2011), and *Aquinas: Moral, Political and Legal Theory* (Oxford University Press, 1998).

Robert G. Kennedy is Professor of Catholic Studies and founding co-director of the Terrence J. Murphy Institute for Catholic Thought, Law and Public Policy at the University of St. Thomas (St. Paul, Minn.) and the author of *The Good that Business Does* (Acton Institute, 2006).

Joseph Koterski, S.J., is Associate Professor of Philosophy, Editor-in-Chief of the *International Philosophical Quarterly*, and the author of *An Introduction to Medieval Philosophy: Basic Concepts* (Wiley-Blackwell, 2009).

Michael Novak (1933–2017) was George Frederick Jewett Scholar in Religion, Philosophy, and Public Policy at the American Enterprise Institute, Distinguished Visiting Professor at Ave Maria University, and co-author of *The Spirit of Democratic Capitalism* (Madison Books, 1990), and *Social Justice Isn't What You Think It Is* (Encounter Books, 2015).

Christopher Wolfe is Distinguished Affiliate Professor at the University of Dallas and Emeritus Professor of Political Science at Marquette University, and the author of *Natural Law Liberalism* (Cambridge University Press, 2006). He is the founding president of the American Public Philosophy Institute.

Nicholas Wolterstorff is Noah Porter Professor Emeritus of Philosophical Theology at Yale University, and was Senior Fellow at the Institute for Advanced Study in Culture, University of Virginia. He is the author of *Justice: Rights and Wrongs* (Princeton University Press, 2008).